SCHOLASTIC

THINKING SKILLS

DAILY BRAIN TEASERS

AGES 9–11

SYLVIA CLEMENTS

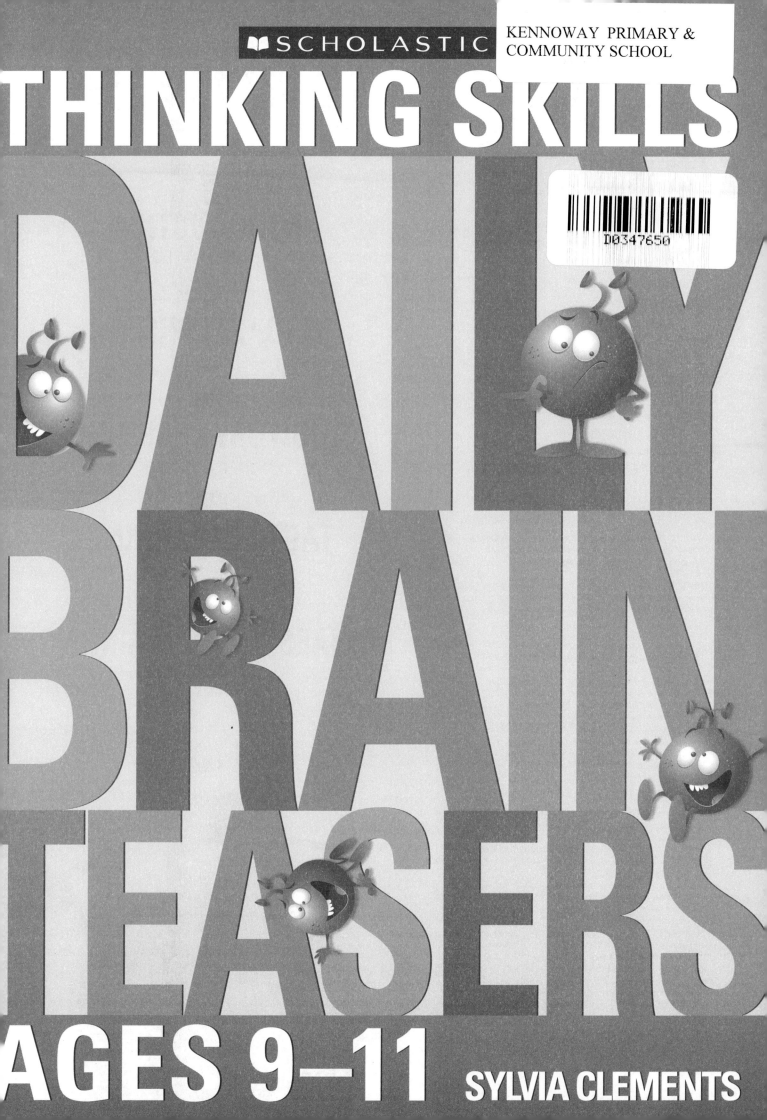

CREDITS

Author
Sylvia Clements

Illustrations
Nick Diggory

Editor
Kim Vernon

Series Designer
Anna Oliwa

Assistant Editor
Niamh O'Carroll

Designer
Melissa Leeke

Text © Sylvia Clements
© 2006 Scholastic Ltd

Designed using Adobe InDesign

Published by Scholastic Ltd
Villiers House, Clarendon Avenue,
Leamington Spa, Warwickshire CV32 5PR

www.scholastic.co.uk

Printed by Bell and Bain Ltd, Glasgow

6789   89012345

British Library Cataloguing-in-Publication Data
A catalogue record for this book is available from the
British Library.

ISBN 0-439-96544-6
ISBN 978-0439-96544-6

The right of Sylvia Clements to be identified as the author
of this work has been asserted by her in accordance with
the Copyright, Designs and Patents Act 1988.

Material from the National Curriculum © The Queen's
Printer and Controller of HMSO. Reproduced under the
terms of HMSO Guidance Note 8.

The publishers wish to thank:
John Coldwell for the use of 'Socks' by John Coldwell
from Scholastic Poetry Anthology Workshop © 1997, John
Coldwell (1997, Scholastic). Co-Sign Communications for
the text extract and illustrations from Sign Language Link:
Desk Edition by Cath Smith © 1999, Cath Smith (1999,
Co-Sign Communications). John Fewings for the use
of 'Jigsaw Pieces – Solutions' by John Fewings from
www.brainboxx.co.uk © 2005, John Fewings (2005,
www.brainboxx.co.uk). Southern Water for a table on
water use from A drip in time – Fact Sheet 2 the Southern
Water WaterWise Teaching Resource © 2002, Southern
Water (2002, Southern Water).

CONTENTS

DAILY BRAINTEASERS FOR AGES 9–11

WHAT IS 'DAILY BRAINTEASERS?'

Daily Brainteasers 9–11 is a collection of over 160 ideas for activities that will develop the five thinking skills highlighted in the National Curriculum: information-processing; reasoning; enquiry; creative thinking; evaluation.

HOW IS IT ORGANISED?

Different children prefer different learning styles: visual (seeing), auditory (hearing), tactile (touching); kinaesthetic (movement). The activities have been grouped into four chapters, each focusing on one of the learning styles.

WHAT DOES EACH BRAINTEASER CONTAIN?

● Each brainteaser details the thinking skill to be developed:

Information processing: collecting, sorting, classifying, sequencing, comparing and contrasting information.

Reasoning: giving reasons for opinions and actions, drawing inferences, making deductions, using precise language to say what they think, making judgements and decisions based on reason/ evidence.

Enquiry: asking relevant questions, posing and defining problems, planning what to do and how to research, predict outcomes and anticipate consequences, testing conclusions and improving ideas.

Creative: generating and extending ideas, suggesting hypotheses, applying imagination, looking for alternative, innovative outcomes.

Evaluation: evaluating information, judging the value of what is read, seen, heard or done, developing criteria for judging the value of their own and others' work or ideas, and developing confidence in their judgements.

(adapted from National Curriculum, 2000)

● Each brainteaser states if there is a link to another learning style.

● It details the subject link – many of the brainteasers are activities that complement objectives in the units from the Year 5 and Year 6 QCA schemes of work.

● Each brainteaser gives suggestions for organisation. Many of the ideas are flexible and can be adapted for teachers' individual situations.

● A list of resources is given and many refer to useful websites (live at the time of publication).

● Instructions for carrying out the brainteasers are given.

● Answers to problems have also been given where appropriate!

The brainteasers are a mixture of original ideas; games or puzzles from ancient civilisations; old favourites, which have been adapted or modernised; and ideas I have picked up during my teaching career, which have proved useful. For the latter, I extend my thanks and acknowledgements to their unknown originators!

HOW SHOULD THEY BE USED?

The brainteasers are a mixture of very quick, short sharp activities that could be carried out in registration, and longer activities to be incorporated into schemes of work.

To achieve successful teaching of thinking skills and, in so doing, produce successful learners – ones who can 'do' as well as 'know – a teacher needs to incorporate thinking skills activities within all areas of the curriculum and develop an ethos in the class whereby children want to learn to think.

ODDS AND EVENS NOUGHTS AND CROSSES

THINKING SKILL: information processing
SUBJECT LINK: mathematics
ORGANISATION: any number of children divided into two teams
RESOURCES: pen and paper for pairs or small groups; class board if playing with the whole class split into two teams

WHAT TO DO

● Draw a noughts and crosses grid.
● One team has the even numbers 2,4,6,8,10 and write in red.
● The other team has the odd numbers 1,3,5,7,9 and write in blue.
● Each team takes it in turn to write one of their numbers in a space on the grid (numbers can be used more than once).

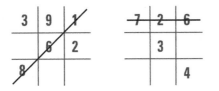

● The aim is to complete a line with the numbers adding up to 15.
● Winning lines can be vertical, horizontal or diagonal.
● The winning team is the one to get the most winning lines.

EMOTION MIND MAP

THINKING SKILL: reasoning
SUBJECT LINK: PSHE
ORGANISATION: whole class and individual
RESOURCES: paper or whiteboard and coloured pens or pencils

WHAT TO DO

● Write 'EMOTIONS' in the middle of the board in a thought cloud.
● As a class, name all the emotions you can think of (happy, sad, angry, cheated, jealous, vindictive, apologetic, frightened). Add new vocabulary and provide definitions.
● Present each emotion as a branch off the central cloud.
● The children copy this as you do it. Individually, children select different emotions on the Emotion Map and write down a phrase that explains what makes them feel that emotion.
● As a class, invite the children to share and discuss their work.
● Reinforce the fact that everyone has a right to think and feel differently and that they should respect this.

A QUESTION OF ART

THINKING SKILL: enquiry
SUBJECT LINK: art
ORGANISATION: small groups
RESOURCES: posters, postcards or books of paintings by a famous artist or artists (ensure that the choice of paintings is thought provoking, www.artchive.com is a useful website for finding information about artists and seeing examples of their work – suggested examples: *The Last Supper* by Leonardo da Vinci; *Figure at Window* by Salvador Dali)

WHAT TO DO

● Write seven question words on the board (who, why, where, what, when, how, which) and give each group a painting.
● Each group should discuss their painting and come up with seven questions – one for each question word.

STORY IMPROVISING

THINKING SKILL: creative
SUBJECT LINK: literacy
LEARNING LINK: tactile
ORGANISATION: whole class
RESOURCES: 30 different objects – anything from a wooden spoon to an umbrella

WHAT TO DO

● Have a bag of objects from which everyone can pick as they come into class. Once seated (preferably in a circle), each child shows the class their object before the activity commences.

● As a class, create a story chain that includes as many of the objects as possible. Choose a volunteer to start the story and include their object. The story then continues around the circle; either in sequence or by individuals volunteering.

● Each storyteller can stop whenever they like and then the next child continues incorporating their own object into the story.

TO VISIT OR NOT TO VISIT?

THINKING SKILL: evaluation
SUBJECT LINK: art, literacy
ORGANISATION: whole class and individual
RESOURCES: multiple copies of leaflets for family attractions such as safari parks or theme parks

WHAT TO DO

● Ask the children to do the following:

● Imagine you are the managing director of a theme park or safari park. Your advertising department has produced a leaflet to inform people about the attraction and persuade them to visit. Draw up a list of things a parent/carer would want to know before deciding whether to go to the chosen location (attractions, directions, opening times, prices, toilet facilities, disabled access, food outlets, gift shops and so on).

● Collate all the individual ideas into a class list to use for assessing the merits of the published leaflets. Decide how to evaluate each feature, for example detailed information could score three points; adequate information could score two points; and insufficient or poorly presented information could score just one point.

● Hand out the leaflets to small groups and carry out an assessment of the leaflets in terms of how useful they are and how they could be improved.

CROSSING A RIVER

THINKING SKILL: reasoning (Variation of classic problem by Alcuin of York)
SUBJECT LINK: mathematics
LEARNING LINK: tactile
ORGANISATION: small groups
RESOURCES: pen and paper or blocks or model people

WHAT TO DO

● Tommy and Trevor are two 11-year-old twins who have been fishing with their father and grandfather. They want to cross the river to find a better place to fish as they have yet to get a bite. There is no bridge and their tiny boat can only hold one adult or two children at any one time. How can they all get across? The boys can row the boat.

● Ask the children to work out the answer to the problem – they can use drawings or models to help visualise the problem.

ANSWER

Tommy and Trevor row across together. Tommy gets out. Trevor rows back. Trevor gets out and Grandpa rows across. He gets out and Tommy rows back across. He collects Trevor and the two boys row back. Trevor gets out and Tommy rows back. Tommy gets out and Dad goes across. Trevor then gets in and goes across to fetch his brother – the two boys finally come across together.
It therefore takes nine trips in total to get them all across!

SYLLABLE HUNT

THINKING SKILL: information processing
SUBJECT LINK: literacy
LEARNING LINK: auditory
ORGANISATION: individual or pairs
RESOURCES: dictionaries; paper and pens; stopwatch

WHAT TO DO

● Revise how to count the number of syllables in a word.

● Challenge the class to look through the dictionaries to see who can find the most four-syllable or five-syllable words in a set time. Start by allowing five minutes and gradually reducing the time as they improve.

● Try this activity with individuals or in pairs – ask the winning pair to explain how they worked as a team.

BOXES

THINKING SKILL: enquiry
SUBJECT LINK: mathematics
ORGANISATION: pairs
RESOURCES: squared paper and pencils.

WHAT TO DO

● Each pair draws a grid of ten by ten dots.
● They take it in turns to join two dots with a line – vertically or horizontally, not diagonally. The dots must be adjoining.

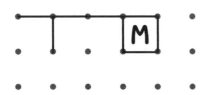

● The aim is to be complete the most boxes. When a child is able to draw the fourth side of the square – that is, complete a box – he/she writes their initial in the box. When a child completes a box, he/she has an extra turn.
● When all the boxes have been completed count up the initials to see who has the most boxes. The total should equal 81.

DREAM HOLDERS

THINKING SKILL: creative
SUBJECT LINK: literacy
LEARNING LINK: tactile
ORGANISATION: individual, ongoing activity
RESOURCES: a collection of containers – boxes, jars and so on; a copy of Roald Dahl's *The BFG* (Puffin books); paper and pens

WHAT TO DO

● To set up this ongoing activity for developing creative thinking, bring in a collection of boxes, jars or other containers – decorate during an art lesson.
● Discuss dreams and memories and think up categories, for example, sad, happy, and scary. Label the containers accordingly and create a permanent space for them somewhere in the classroom.
● Ask the class to recall a memory or dream to write down and store in the jars. Thoughts may be shared or remain anonymous. Individuals can choose which type of dream or memory to recall.
● Return to this activity on other occasions.

ODD-ONE-OUT

THINKING SKILL: reasoning
SUBJECT LINK: geography
ORGANISATION: pairs
RESOURCES: atlases; odd-one-out statements on the board

WHAT TO DO

● Write up the following list on the board.
● In pairs, find the odd-one-out for each question.
● Give the reason why.
● Discuss the answers and the reasons as a class.

Atlantic, Indian, Pacific, Mediterranean

Lima, Buenos Aires, Santiago, Pretoria

Sri Lanka, Madagascar, Sardinia, South Korea

Niger, Amazon, Zambezi, Nile

Appalachians, Andes, Alps, Rocky

A   B   C   D

ANSWERS

Mediterranean – is a sea, the others are oceans.
Pretoria – capital of South Africa, the others are capital cities of countries in South America (Peru, Argentina, Chile).
South Korea – the others are all islands, surrounded by sea.
Amazon – this river is in South America. The others are all rivers in Africa.
The Alps is the only European range. The others are all in the Americas (Eastern USA, Western South America, Western North America).
A) This is the flag of China, which is in the continent of Asia; the other flags are all European flags (Switzerland, Norway and United Kingdom).

COLOUR NAMES

THINKING SKILL: creative
SUBJECT LINK: art, literacy
ORGANISATION: pairs
RESOURCES: paint colour charts with the colour names removed; scissors; mounting paper or card; glue

WHAT TO DO

● Give each group a colour chart.
● Look at the different names for colours on the chart.
● Choose one example of a colour, such as

blue, and think of a new name for the colour, in the style of the colour charts, for example (for blue): oceans, forget-me-nots, peacocks, blueberries, sky, sea, sadness.

● Cut the colour cards up, keeping the colour boxes only, and arrange in patterns, giving each colour an appropriate name and writing it neatly below each strip.

● Allow the use of reference books such as wild flower books if required to expand knowledge.

BIG CAT, LITTLE CAT

THINKING SKILL: reasoning
SUBJECT LINK: mathematics
LEARNING LINK: tactile
ORGANISATION: individual
RESOURCES: cards with each of the following names written on: Felix, Fifi, Casper, Bobby, Poppy; paper and pen

WHAT TO DO

● Read these sentences and list the cats in order of their weights, starting with the heaviest.

The ferocious feline Felix is heavier than the feeble Fifi.

Crafty Casper weighs more than Bobby but less than Poppy.

● Arrange and order the cards to test out your ideas.

ANSWER
Felix, Poppy, Casper, Bobby, Fifi.

PLACE CHAINS

THINKING SKILL: enquiry
SUBJECT LINK: geography
ORGANISATION: pairs
RESOURCES: atlases; pen and paper

WHAT TO DO

● Provide the class with a starter country, for example, England.

● In pairs, using an atlas of the world, challenge the children to make the longest chain of countries, each country beginning with the last letter of the country before. No country can be used more than once. Allocate points for each correct country. (You may want to allocate an obscure number of points for each correct answer to incorporate maths skills too!) A chain using England as the starter might be: England – Denmark – Kenya – Austria – Australia and so on.

● Vary this game by using names of towns, rivers and so on.

TIME FACTS

THINKING SKILL: information processing
SUBJECT LINK: mathematics, geography
LEARNING LINK: auditory
ORGANISATION: individual or pairs (mixed ability)
RESOURCES: paper and pen; calculator

WHAT TO DO

● Establish the following time facts together:

60 seconds = 1 minute
60 minutes = 1 hour
24 hours = 1 day
7 days = 1 week
2 weeks = 1 fortnight
365 days = 1 year
366 days = 1 leap year (every 4 years); 2004 was the last leap year.
30 days in September, April, June, November.
31 days in Jan, March, May, July, August, October, December.
28 days in February (29 in a leap year).
12 months = 1 year
100 years = 1 century

● Challenge the class to create 'Time Fact Statements', using this information base, such as:

There are 86400 seconds in 1 day. (60 × 60 × 24)

There were 31622400 seconds in 2004. (86400 × 366 days)

● Allow a set time, then share all the statements and encourage the class to check their validity.

● Record and display the best examples.

WORDS WITHIN WORDS

THINKING SKILL: enquiry
SUBJECT LINK: literacy
ORGANISATION: individual
RESOURCES: pen and paper

WHAT TO DO

● Write a long word, such as 'philosophical' or 'surveillance' on the board.
● Challenge the class to find as many words as they can, using letters from within the given word. They may use each letter only once.
● Decide on a scoring system, such as one point for two-, three- or four-letter words, two points for five-letter words and five points for words with more than five letters.

TV GUIDE QUIZ

THINKING SKILL: enquiry, information processing
SUBJECT LINK: maths
ORGANISATION: individual
RESOURCES: TV page from a newspaper (one for each child)

WHAT TO DO

● Each child should create a set number of questions about the TV programmes shown on the page for their neighbour to answer. They could ask questions such as:

How long is the news on Channel 4?
How long is there between the end of programme x which starts at 6:00pm and the start of programme y?
Which is the longest programme on BBC1?

SPEED GRID REFERENCES

THINKING SKILL: information processing
SUBJECT LINK: geography
ORGANISATION: small groups
RESOURCES: OS maps

WHAT TO DO

● Recap how to use four-figure grid references. Teach the phrase, *Along the corridor and up the stairs*, as a reminder that they should locate the horizontal points first and then the vertical.
● Write ten four-figure grid references, which relate to features on the map for the groups to find. Set the challenge against the clock.

● As groups finish, check their answers and then allow them to create their own grid references for others to find while waiting for everyone to finish.
● Encourage them to use the key to find the meanings of any abbreviations and features.

ALPHABET POEM

THINKING SKILL: creative
SUBJECT LINK: literacy
ORGANISATION: individual or pairs
RESOURCES: pen and paper

WHAT TO DO

● Write the alphabet down the left-hand side of a piece of paper.
● For each letter, the class should come up with an imaginative adjective, noun and verb (in the present continuous, for example arguing, bouncing).
● Share the findings and agree on the best examples to use to make up an imaginative alphabet poem.

HOMONYM HUNTING

THINKING SKILL: information processing
SUBJECT LINK: literacy
ORGANISATION: individual
RESOURCES: pen and paper; dictionaries

WHAT TO DO

● Challenge the class to scan their dictionaries to find as many homonyms as they can (a homonym being a word spelt or pronounced the same as another but with a different meaning, for example: beach/beech; assistance/assistants; baron/barren; brewed/brood).
● Secondly, ask the class to see who can find words with the highest number of different meanings. For example, Bully: 1. Person coercing others by fear; 2. Putting ball into play in hockey; 3. Corned beef.

CRACK THE CODE

THINKING SKILL: enquiry
SUBJECT LINK: science
ORGANISATION: individual or pairs
RESOURCES: paper and pen

WHAT TO DO

● Write the following puzzle on the board for the class to solve.
● Each letter below stands for the name of something. What do they stand for and what should the last three letters be?

M V E M J S ? ? ?

ANSWER
They are the initials of the planets: Mercury, Venus, Earth, Mars, Jupiter, Saturn. So the remaining three letters are: U for Uranus, N for Neptune, and P for Pluto.

ONE-MINUTE ARTISTS

THINKING SKILL: creative
SUBJECT LINK: art
ORGANISATION: whole class divided into two teams
RESOURCES: whiteboard; pens; a set of word or phrase cards to serve as picture suggestion (suggestions for the cards – hot dog, earthquake, sandpit); one-minute sand timer

WHAT TO DO

● Split the class into two teams. Decide how many rounds the game is going to involve (depending on time). Use this to choose which children are going to be the artists for the game. For example, five rounds requires five artists for each team.
● The first artist from Team A comes to the board, is shown a picture card, the one-minute timer is set and the artist attempts to draw the word or phrase.
● No letters, numbers or gesticulation for partially correct answers is allowed.
● The rest of the team call out their answers. If the correct answer is given within a minute, the team scores a point. If not, one suggestion can be taken from the opposing team. If they are correct, they get the point.

THE HOLE PROBLEM

THINKING SKILL: enquiry
SUBJECT LINK: mathematics (logical)
ORGANISATION: individual
RESOURCES: puzzle board

WHAT TO DO

● Write up this problem on the daily puzzle board:

A man digs a round hole that is 3 metres deep and has a diameter of 1.5 metres. How much soil is in the hole?

ANSWER
None, the hole is empty. The volume of soil that has been removed from the hole however is calculated by working out the volume of a cylinder with radius 0.75m and height 3m. The volume of a cylinder is L × pi × r² = 5.3035714285714235.

CALCULATION BINGO

THINKING SKILL: evaluation
SUBJECT LINK: mathematics
ORGANISATION: pairs
RESOURCES: pen and paper; two die

WHAT TO DO

● Each player writes down the numbers 0, 1, 2, 3, 4, 5, 6, 7, 8, 9, 10, 11, 12 in a line, spaced clearly.
● Decide who is to begin by rolling the die, the person rolling the highest number starts.
● The aim is to be the first player to cross off all their numbers.
● The first player rolls the two die, and then crosses off both numbers and the numbers they can make by adding, subtracting, multiplying or dividing the two numbers rolled.
● For example; rolling a 4 and a 3 would mean crossing off 3, 4, 1 (4 – 3 = 1), 7 (4 + 3 = 7), 12 (3 × 4 = 12).

SITUATIONS

THINKING SKILL: reasoning
SUBJECT LINK: PSHE/citizenship
ORGANISATION: small groups
RESOURCES: situation cards; pens

WHAT TO DO

● Draw four figures on the board, representing two parents/carers and a brother and sister (about ten-years-old).

● Draw an empty speech bubble and an empty thought bubble above each head.

● Hand out situation cards to each group and ask them to discuss and agree what each person might be saying and what they might be thinking during the described situation.

> Suggestions for the situation cards:
> *The children went to the shopping centre after school without letting anyone know where they were or what they were doing.*
> *One of the children has broken a sentimental ornament and has not owned up.*
> *The children refuse to do their chores but want an increase in pocket money.*

INVENTION DETECTION

THINKING SKILL: enquiry
SUBJECT LINK: science
ORGANISATION: pairs
RESOURCES: encyclopaedias; non-fiction books; CD-ROMs; the internet

WHAT TO DO

● As a class, produce a list of inventions (telephone, food mixer, chocolate, hot water bottle and so on).

● Allocate one invention to each pair, whose task it is to find out:
  ● Who invented it?
  ● When was it invented?
  ● Where was it invented?
  ● Why was it invented?
  ● How did the original version work?

● Share the research findings as a whole class at a later date.

THE HOMONYM CHALLENGE

THINKING SKILL: enquiry
SUBJECT LINK: literacy
ORGANISATION: teams of four or five children
RESOURCES: dictionaries; pens and paper; whiteboard and two different coloured pens

WHAT TO DO

● Write on the board the list of homonyms (red) and definitions (blue) shown below, splitting the words from the meanings.

aloud (with noise)	allowed (permitted)
assistance (waiting on)	assistants (those who help out)
coarse (rough)	course (route)
cygnet (young swan)	signet (a seal)
desert (to abandon)	dessert (pudding)
hew (to cut down)	hue (colour)
incidence (single happening)	incidents (events)
meddle (interfere)	medal (a token)
residence (place of abode)	residents (citizens)
yoke (yellow of an egg)	yolk (collar for oxen)

● The teams should match up each homonym with its correct meaning. Allow ten minutes to complete this.

● The children should then prepare sentences incorporating examples of the homonyms to challenge the other teams.

● Each team scores:
  ● two points for a correctly structured sentence
  ● one point if they outwit the team they challenge.
  ● If a team suggests an incorrect homonym one point is deducted from their score.
  ● If they are correct they score two points.

● Each team starts with ten points. Teams choose who they wish to challenge. The winner is the team with the most points after a set number of challenges.

NEWS HOUNDS

THINKING SKILL: enquiry

SUBJECT LINK: geography, citizenship

ORGANISATION: pairs and whole class

RESOURCES: quality daily newspaper (appropriately censored); map of the world; map pins or flag pins; empty project book; scissors; glue; highlighter pen; class list

WHAT TO DO:

● This ongoing activity requires a dedicated area of the classroom.

● Put up a world map and on a table next to it supply a pot of map pins (which can be written on with numbers) and the other resources. Give the display a title such as 'News Around the World'.

● Pair up the children and allocate a day for each pair to carry out the activity. Each day provide a daily newspaper for perusal.

● Each pair has to choose and read an interesting international news article. They then locate the country featured and mark it with a map pin. The pair cut out the article, stick it in the project book, date and number it. They put the corresponding number on their map pin.

● At the end of each week, pairs state which country their story came from and relate the news article to the class. Provide explanations if necessary. After a while, discuss any patterns emerging on the map in relation to the location and nature of the articles chosen.

ROMAN NUMERALS

THINKING SKILL: reasoning

SUBJECT LINK: mathematics, history

ORGANISATION: individual

RESOURCES: paper and pen

WHAT TO DO

● Recap Roman numbers and the seven letters of the alphabet they used as numerals.

I	=	1
V	=	5
X	=	10
L	=	50
C	=	100
D	=	500
M	=	1000

a. $IV + VI =$ b. $VII + CXVI =$
c. $XXV - VI =$ d. $V + V + V =$
e. $MD - CCL =$ f. $LVI - XXV =$

● Ask the children to work out in Roman numerals:

   a. the year of their birth
   b. the current year
   c. 1999.

● Ask them to use history books or a class timeline to write some famous dates in Roman numerals for the rest of the class to work out and state what the significance of the date was.

● As an additional task, ask the children to find out when Roman numerals are used in modern times.

ANSWERS

a. X   b. CXXIII   c. XIX
d. XV e. MCCL   f. XXXI

One way of writing 1999 = MDCCCCLXXXXIX

Roman numerals are used for: copyright dates on television programmes and videos; to show the hours on some analogue clocks and watches; on a book's preliminary pages before the main page numbering; the numbering of the Olympic Games; monarchs and popes, for example, Henry VIII; public buildings, monuments and gravestones, sometimes have Roman numeral dates on when the inscription is in Latin.

PAIRS

THINKING SKILL: information processing

SUBJECT LINK: any

ORGANISATION: groups

RESOURCES: sets of 30 blank cards for each group (cut a sheet of A4 card into ten equal cards)

WHAT TO DO

● Ask the groups to make a set of 'pairs' cards according to a chosen theme – for example animals and their young, pairs of historical characters, or books and their authors. They will need to think of 15 pairs and write them on the blank cards.

● When the set of cards has been made, the cards should be shuffled and spread out on a table face down, around which the group sits.

● Players take turns to turn over two cards, in an attempt to reveal a pair.

● If they locate a pair, they collect the pair and keep it. If not, they turn the two cards back over in the positions they found them. The next player then attempts to find a pair.

● The winner is the player who holds the most pairs once all the cards have been picked.

● Groups can swap sets of cards on different occasions.

PROBABILITY CHALLENGE

THINKING SKILL: information processing
SUBJECT LINK: mathematics
ORGANISATION: pairs and whole class
RESOURCES: dice; pen and paper

WHAT TO DO

● In pairs, each player chooses a number that can be made with two dice. Then each person rolls two dice 20 times to try to get that number. Each time they do get their number they record it with a tally mark. The person who gets his or her number the most times wins.

● Next collate the results – ask who chose, 2,3,4,5,6,7,8,9,10,11,12 and record how many times each person's number came up.

● Ask the class to work out which number is likely to be the best choice, based on the premise that each combination of numbers is equally likely on a roll. Check whether this was true for the class's experiment.

ANSWERS

There is only 1 way to roll a 2 (1,1).
There are 2 ways to roll a 3 (1,2; 2,1).
There are 3 ways to roll a 4 (1,3; 2,2; 3,1).
There are 4 ways to roll a 5 (1,4; 2,3; 3,2; 4,1).
There are 5 ways to roll a 6 (1,5; 2,4; 3,3; 4,2; 5,1).
There are 6 ways to roll a 7 (1,6; 2,5; 3,4; 4,3; 5,2; 6,1).
There are 5 ways to roll an 8 (2,6; 3,5; 4,4; 5,3; 6,2).
There are 4 ways to roll a 9 (3,6; 4,5; 5,4; 6,3).
There are 3 ways to roll a 10 (4,6; 5,5; 6,4).
There are 2 ways to roll a 11 (5,6; 6,5).
There is only 1 way to roll a 12 (6,6).

Adding up the above, there are 36 possible combinations. Out of 36 rolls, 2 is likely to come up once, 3 is likely to come up twice and so on. So,7 is the best choice as there are 6 ways to roll a 7.

HOW FAR DO THEY TRAVEL?

THINKING SKILL: information processing
SUBJECT LINK: mathematics, geography
ORGANISATION: individual
RESOURCES: pen and paper

WHAT TO DO

● Write up the following for the children to work out during registration:

● All the teachers live within 30 miles of the school but how far exactly do they have to travel to get to school each day?

● Mr Green lives 15 miles south of school.
● Mrs Grey lives 20 miles north of Mr Brown.
● Miss Red lives 5 miles south of Mr Green.
● Mr Brown lives 10 miles north of Miss Red.
● Mr Yellow lives 15 miles south of Mr Brown.

ANSWERS

Tell the children to draw out the answers to help them find the solution:
Mr Green = 15 miles south of the school
Mrs Grey = 10 miles north of the school
Miss Red = 20 miles south of the school
Mr Brown = 10 miles south of the school
Mr Yellow = 25 miles south of the school

PLACES

THINKING SKILL: information processing, enquiry
SUBJECT LINK: geography, mathematics
ORGANISATION: whole class, then pairs
RESOURCES: map of the British Isles; compass points

WHAT TO DO

● Create a mind map of the main towns and cities in the British Isles. Complete an eight- or sixteen-point compass.

● Ask the children to work out in which direction towns or cities lie in relation to each other.

Nottingham lies _____ of Manchester
Dundee lies _____ of Edinburgh
Plymouth lies _____ of Bristol
Newcastle lies _____ of Edinburgh
Sheffield lies _____ of Swansea
Brighton lies _____ of Bournemouth
Leeds lies _____ of Lincoln

● Ask them, if a plane flew directly east from Aberystwyth which towns or cities would it pass over?

● Ask pairs to set similar questions for other pairs.

ALL ABOUT ME

THINKING SKILL: enquiry
SUBJECT LINK: literacy
ORGANISATION: individuals then pairs
RESOURCES: pen and paper; copy of an interview from a magazine or comic or the internet (an excellent example of an author interview can be found on www.roalddahl.com)

WHAT TO DO

● Talk about interviews that the children may have seen in comics or magazines or on the internet. Discuss the sort of people who get interviewed and the sort of questions they get asked.
● Complete an interview questionnaire using the following statement starters as well as any others the class can suggest:

If I have time to myself I like to….
I am happiest when….
My greatest weakness is …
If I could pass any law it would be…
If I could be someone else I would be…
My proudest moment was…
The best day of my life so far was…
My worst habit is…
If I had to change something about myself it would be…
Not a lot of people know this but…

FASHION DESIGNER CHALLENGE

THINKING SKILL: creative
SUBJECT LINK: art
ORGANISATION: individual
RESOURCES: pencils; pens; paper outline of socks or pants

WHAT TO DO

● Brainstorm a list of famous people – contemporary and historical. Write each one on a slip of paper and place them in a container. Everyone in the class picks a slip and keeps the identity of their person secret.
● Choose an item of clothing such as trousers or socks and prepare a blank outline for the class to use.
● Children create an appropriate design for the clothing of their famous person. At the end of the set time, the designs are displayed and other children guess who the garment was designed for.

HOW MUCH WILL I NEED?

THINKING SKILL: reasoning
SUBJECT LINK: mathematics
ORGANISATION: individual
RESOURCES: pen and paper

WHAT TO DO

● Ask the children to work out the following:

The following recipe for chocolate brownies makes twelve squares. If you are having seven people round to tea and you want each person to have three squares, work out how to change the recipe to make sure you cook enough biscuits for everyone.

50g of plain chocolate
110g butter
2 beaten for eggs
225g of sugar
50g of plain flour
1 teaspoon of baking powder
¼ teaspoon of salt
110g of chopped nuts

ANSWER
7 people + yourself makes 8 people.
3 squares each is a total of 8 × 3 = 24
The recipe must be doubled.

THE WONDERS OF WATER

THINKING SKILL: enquiry
SUBJECT LINK: science
ORGANISATION: whole class, then groups
RESOURCES: large sheet of paper and marker pens

WHAT TO DO

● Briefly discuss where our water comes from and what happens to waste water. Explain that clean water is precious and that we need to use it wisely because there are about 450 million people in the world who are facing water shortages.

● Take a large piece of paper and draw a large drop of water in the centre, inside which write WATER. Around the outside of this droplet, brainstorm as many ways of using water as you can. Write these in one colour as branches from the water droplet.

● Take a second colour and draw a branch from each water usage suggestion and state how the quantity of water used could be reduced, for example, use a bowl of water to wash vegetables, turn off the tap while brushing teeth, have a shower instead of a bath.

● Pool the groups' ideas and expand on these by visiting one of many useful websites that address the subject, such as www.environment-agency.gov.uk

MAKE THE NUMBER

THINKING SKILL: information processing
SUBJECT LINK: mathematics
ORGANISATION: individual
RESOURCES: pen and paper

WHAT TO DO

● Set a target number (for example, 473) and challenge the class to find as many ways of reaching that target as possible, using all four operations (+,–, × and ÷).

YOUR MOVE

THINKING SKILL: reasoning
SUBJECT LINK: mathematics
LEARNING LINK: tactile
ORGANISATION: individual
RESOURCES: squared paper; ten card counters and felt tip pens

WHAT TO DO

● Prepare a four by four grid and make ten counters that will fit onto the squares. The counters should be one colour on one side and a contrasting colour on the other side.

● Set up the counters as in the diagram:

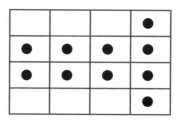

● Turn all the counters over in 10 moves. A counter is turned over when another counter jumps it, either diagonally or straight over.

QUEEN VICTORIA'S FAMILY TREE

THINKING SKILL: enquiry
SUBJECT LINK: history
ORGANISATION: individuals, then whole class
RESOURCES: Queen Victoria's family tree on board; pen and paper

WHAT TO DO

● Discuss with the class the meaning of niece, nephew, aunt, uncle, first cousin, second cousin and so on.

● Draw up Queen Victoria's family tree on the board and ask the children a few questions such as:

  ● Who was Queen Victoria's father?
  ● How many children did she have?
  ● Who were Queen Victoria's uncles?

● Now ask the children to create ten more questions about this family tree to share with the class

SPLIT THE WORD

THINKING SKILL: information processing
SUBJECT LINK: literacy
ORGANISATION: individual
RESOURCES: pen and paper; dictionaries

WHAT TO DO

Ask the children to find how many words of three or more letters are contained within each of the words listed below, without rearranging the letters:

> restoration
> tangerine
> complimentary
> wardrobe
> drawing
> coincidentally
> sentimental
> whatever
> whenever
> scarecrow

ANSWERS

rest, rat, ration
tan, tang, anger
lime, men, tar, compliment
ward, robe, rob, war,
draw, raw, win, wing
coin, dent, den, tall, tally, coincide, incident
sent, time, men, mental, sentiment
what, hat, ate, ever, eve, hate,
when, hen, ever, eve, never
scare, scar, are, crow, row, car, care

NOW TRY THIS

Use a dictionary to see who can find the word with the most other words (three letters or more) contained within it – without any letters being rearranged.

ART POLL

THINKING SKILL: evaluation
SUBJECT LINK: art
LEARNING LINK: auditory
ORGANISATION: whole class
RESOURCES: art print posters by a wide range of artists from a range of different movements – perhaps Aboriginal art to Renoir to Jackson Pollack; speech bubble and pen

WHAT TO DO

Display the posters and allocate a number or letter to each. Ask the children to study the pictures and carefully choose their favourite and least favourite print.

They should complete a speech bubble expressing in it their opinion; *I like/dislike this painting because...* and then attach it to the edge of the appropriate poster. Afterwards speech bubbles can be read out and compared to see if there was any consensus of opinion. This exercise can be used as a springboard into a range of discussions about art and artists.

WORD LADDERS

THINKING SKILL: information processing
SUBJECT LINK: literacy
ORGANISATION: individual or pairs
RESOURCES: dictionaries; pen and paper

WHAT TO DO

● As a class, agree on a pair of words (perhaps synonyms or antonyms) with about nine or ten letters in each, for example, observant and regardful.
● Write the words vertically down a page, one on the left-hand side and one down the right-hand side.
● The challenge is to find words to fit between the pairs of letters, using dictionaries (as this will help to increase vocabulary). For example, you could have oar or observer or occupier between the 'o' and the 'r' but the highest score would be for oceanographer!
● Award one point for each letter of each correct word formed. The winner is the child or pair with the highest point score for all nine or ten new words.

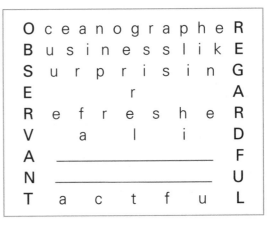

HOW MUCH WATER DO WE USE?

THINKING SKILL: enquiry
SUBJECT LINK: science
ORGANISATION: small groups
RESOURCES: water usage table, calculator, pen and paper

WHAT TO DO

● Ask the children to calculate approximately how many litres of water they think their family uses in either a day or a week based on the figures in the table. They will have to consider how many people in the family, how often on average they use the toilet, have a bath, clean teeth and so on.

● Ask them to create their own table to help with the calculation. They can use a column to record the number of times each activity is carried out daily and a further column to allow you calculate the total for each activity.

Activity	Daily amount used in litres
Kitchen	24
Washing clothes	32
Dishwasher	1.6
Toilet flushing	49.6
Garden	6.4
Bath	24
Shower	8
Personal washing	14.4

[table source: www.southernwater.co.uk]

Note: The average amount of water consumed by individuals per day in this country is 160 litres. (www.southernwater.co.uk : Education RESOURCES A Drip in Time Fact Sheet 2)

RESPECT!

THINKING SKILL: reasoning, evaluation
SUBJECT LINK: citizenship
LEARNING LINK: auditory
ORGANISATION: whole class
RESOURCES: digital cameras

WHAT TO DO

● Encourage the children to take digital photographs of evidence of vandalism, graffiti, litter, pollution and damage to property and nature areas both in and around school. This can be done as a homework exercise or on an organised school walk (Safety issue: ensure that the children are supervised.)

● Make a large collage display of the photographs and use them as a stimulus for discussion and writing about the impacts of people's actions. Surround the collage with some of the key words that come out of the discussions.

TIMES TABLE KIM'S GAME

THINKING SKILL: information processing
SUBJECT LINK: mathematics
ORGANISATION: whole class
RESOURCES: whiteboard

WHAT TO DO

● Choose one or two of the times tables that the class needs to practise. Ask them to recite the tables and as they do so write the answers randomly all over the board.

● When all the answers are on the board, point to numbers at random and ask for the sum. Go through all the numbers.

● Next ask the children to put their heads down and close their eyes.

● While they are not looking, rub off one of the numbers. Call *Ready!* The children look up and put their hand up as soon as they have spotted the missing number and can tell you which two numbers multiplied together gave that answer.

● Continue doing this until all the numbers have been rubbed from the board.

REBUS PUZZLES

THINKING SKILL: creative
SUBJECT LINK: literacy, art
ORGANISATION: whole class, then individual
RESOURCES: whiteboard; pens and paper; the internet

WHAT TO DO

● A rebus is a representation of a word, phrase or a name using pictures, as below:

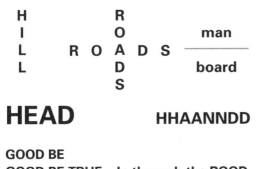

● These simple examples are representations of downhill, crossroads, man overboard, big head, hand-in-hand, too good to be true, in through the back door and unfinished business. To create these puzzles there are a number of techniques that can be used:

> including clue words,
> varying the size of the letters appropriately,
> varying the style of the writing,
> consideration of the positioning of the words,
> placing a line between words to indicate 'over', 'above' or 'below,
> hiding words within words,
> writing the words several times according to the phrase being represented,
> using lines and arrows,
> writing the words backwards or sloping,
> missing out letters.

● Put the above rebus puzzles on the board for the children to solve. Go over how they have been created, then see if they can create their own rebus puzzles for the following words and phrases:

> waterfall   top secret
> tickled pink   half-hearted
> downhill   once in a blue moon
> overboard   broken glass

JUNK FOOD BATTLESHIPS

THINKING SKILL: information processing
SUBJECT LINK: mathematics, citizenship, science
LEARNING LINK: tactile
ORGANISATION: pairs
RESOURCES: squared paper; coloured pens

WHAT TO DO

● This game is based on the traditional game of battleships. Instead of ships as targets, the children create junk food targets.
● Each player draws a twelve by twelve grid and writes the letters A to L along the bottom (one letter for each square) and 1 to 12 up the side (one number for each square). They secretly position their 'Junk Food fleet' on the grid, agreeing on a chosen colour for each. For example:

1 × greasy bag of chips

2 × chocolate coated sticky donuts

3 × fizzy cans of drink

4 × bags of crisps

5 × chewy sweets

● No two items can be adjacent.
● Without letting his or her opponent see, each player takes turns in guessing a junk food location (B7 for example). If it is a hit, the opponent has to declare, *Hit, sticky donut* for example. This will mean that the player knows they have hit a four square target and can set about destroying the whole donut!
● It is advisable for each player to record their own suggestions in one colour (recording a cross for a miss, or the initial of the item for a hit) and their opponents in another.
● The winner is the first player to 'wipe out' all their opponent's junk food.

ANAGRAM ANTICS

THINKING SKILL: information processing
SUBJECT LINK: literacy
ORGANISATION: individual
RESOURCES: pen and paper; dictionaries

WHAT TO DO

● Ask the children to rearrange words to find another correctly spelt word using the same letters in the word.
● Give some easy examples to start with, for example:

  lamp = palm
  snoop = spoon
  north = thorn
  petal = plate
  chain = china

● Now ask them to try these:

  auction   teaching   asleep
  potion   sister   wolves
  kitchen   rustic   height
  parties

> **ANSWERS**
> caution   cheating   please
> option   resist   vowels
> thicken   citrus   eighth
> pirates

NOW TRY THIS

See how many words you can find which have anagrams hidden within them. Challenge the class to find your hidden words.

MYSTERY JOURNEYS

THINKING SKILL: enquiry
SUBJECT LINK: geography
ORGANISATION: pairs
RESOURCES: atlases; whiteboards and pens

WHAT TO DO

● Ensure that the children are able to identify the different features shown on the map used (capital cities, rivers and so on).
● Each pair should decide on a starting place and a destination and plan a flight between the two places. They should provide clues to the route by detailing capital cities, bodies of water, mountains and so on (but not country names).
● Pairs read out their routes so that the class can determine the country of origin and the destination.

NUMBER NAME GAME

THINKING SKILL: information processing
SUBJECT LINK: mathematics
ORGANISATION: individual
RESOURCES: number sentence puzzles

WHAT TO DO

● Ask the children to solve the number sentences by working out what the missing words are. They should use their knowledge of numbers to find logical solutions to the problems. Provide an example to demonstrate how the number sentences work, such as:

> 26 L of the A
> when completed this reads '26 Letters of the Alphabet'.
>
> 366 D in a L Y   6 W of H the E
> 8 L on an O   60 S in a M
> 60 M in an H   360 D in a C
> 100 Y in a C   12 D of C
> 12 S of the Z   29 D in F in a LY
> 9 P in the S S   12 in a D
> 13 in a B D   9 L of a C
> 7 C in a R

> **ANSWERS**
> 366 Days in a Leap Year.
> 6 Wives of Henry the Eighth.
> 8 Legs on an Octopus.
> 60 Seconds in a Minute.
> 60 Minutes in an Hour.
> 360 Degrees in a Circle.
> 100 Years in a Century.
> 12 Days of Christmas.
> 12 Signs of the Zodiac.
> 29 Days in February in a Leap Year.
> 9 Planets in the Solar System.
> 12 in a Dozen.
> 13 in a Baker's Dozen.
> 9 Lives of a Cat.
> 7 Colours in a Rainbow.

PICTURE THIS

THINKING SKILL: information processing
SUBJECT LINK: art, literacy – speaking and listening
LEARNING LINK: auditory
ORGANISATION: whole class
RESOURCES: pictures; pens, coloured pencils and paper

WHAT TO DO

● Choose a volunteer to be the describer. The describer stands at the front of the class and is given a picture to describe to the rest of the class. Nobody else should be able to see the picture.
● Everyone else listens to the description of the picture and draws what is being described.
● At the end of the description, the picture is revealed and everyone holds up his or her versions. The teacher picks the best match.
● The owner of the winning picture is the next describer (or can nominate another child).

DOUBLETS

THINKING SKILL: information processing
SUBJECT LINK: literacy
LEARNING LINK: tactile
ORGANISATION: individual
RESOURCES: squared card or paper; coloured pencils

WHAT TO DO

● As well as being a writer, Lewis Carroll (Charles Dodgson) the author of Alice in Wonderland was also a mathematician, logician and word game enthusiast. In an article in *Vanity Fair* on 29 March 1879, the readers were introduced to a new kind of puzzle, the doublet. These are now known as word ladders. The aim is to take a pair of words of the same length and link them with a chain of words, changing only one letter at a time – making the chain as short as possible.
● Write these 'doublets' on the board for the class to try:

CAT – DOG
SHOE – BOOT
MORE – LESS
CAMP – SITE
WHEAT – BREAD
COLD – WARM

● Create a set of letter cards – at least two for each consonant and several for each vowel – and replace one letter at a time in the sequence. Alternatively use Scrabble pieces, or other similar pieces.

> **ANSWERS**
> CAT – COT – COG - DOG
> SHOE – SHOT – SOOT – BOOT
> MORE – LORE – LOSE – LOSS
> CAMP – CAME – SAME – SATE – SITE
> WHEAT– CHEAT– CHEAP– CHEEP– CREEP
> –CREED– BREED – BREAD
> COLD – CORD – WORD – WORM – WARM

NOW TRY THIS

Ask the children to make up some doublets for their friends to work out. They will need to tell their friends how many links are allowed to make the chain.

HISTORY HANGMAN

THINKING SKILL: information processing
SUBJECT LINK: history, geography
ORGANISATION: whole class
RESOURCES: word cards; board

WHAT TO DO

● Choose one child to be the 'hangman'. He/she selects a word card and draws up an appropriate number of dashes – one to represent each letter in the word (using word cards avoids spelling errors!) The cards should contain words relevant to current topics in geography or history.
● The children then take turns in selecting letters to try. Correct guesses are inserted on the correct dash. Incorrect guesses are recorded in a 'letter dump' at the side of underneath the dashes and one part of the victim is added to the noose!
● If the class guess the word correctly before the body is completed they win. However, if a complete body is drawn from the hangman's noose, the hangman wins. Decide on the parts of the body to be drawn BEFORE starting the game – one head, one line for a body, one line for each arm and each leg and one line for each foot – this gives a total of eight wrong attempts before hanging.

FOLLOW ME

THINKING SKILL: information processing
SUBJECT LINK: mathematics or any curriculum area
LEARNING LINK: visual
ORGANISATION: whole class
RESOURCES: a stopwatch; a set of 'Follow Me' cards (prepared by the teacher as detailed below)

WHAT TO DO

● You will need exactly one card for each child – complete the cards with maths problems you wish your class to practise. For example, a range of times tables:

> I am 48
> Follow me if you are 6 × 12

> I am 72
> Follow me if you are 3 × 12

● When preparing the cards, make sure that the number you begin with is answered by another card's sum.
● Hand out one card to each child.
● Select someone use the stopwatch to time how long the game takes.
● The first player stands and does an action (for example, patting their head) as they read out their card. *I am 48. Follow me if you are 6 × 12.*
● The person who 'is' the answer stands up, follows the action and reads out the answer, *I am 72.* He/she must then do a new action and say (for example) *Follow me if you are 3 × 12.*
● The aim is to get back to the person who started as quickly as possible.
● To play again, collect in the cards, shuffle and hand them out again.
● Keep a record of how long each game took to provide a goal for the next game. Make up different sets of 'Follow Me' cards.

NOW TRY THIS

Make different sets of cards to practise different concepts, for example, French vocabulary.

MAGIC BOX

THINKING SKILL: creative
SUBJECT LINK: literacy
LEARNING LINK: tactile
ORGANISATION: individual
RESOURCES: a copy of the poem, 'The Magic Box' by Kit Wright, which can be found in *Cat Among the Pigeons* (Puffin Books), as well as in anthologies such as *The Word Party* (Macmillan), *Poetry* (Macmillan English), and *Jumpstart* (Poetry Society) by Cliff Yates; a box that can be decorated and made into a 'magic box', during an art lesson (it is important that every member of the class contributes to this to ensure shared 'ownership'); strips of card and metallic pens

WHAT TO DO

● Read the poem and discuss the concept of a magic box into which anything that springs from the imagination can be placed. Which ideas do they like and why?
● Develop ideas for the class's own box. Make the box during an art session using brightly coloured foils, shiny materials and so on and create a special place for it in the class, possibly on a piece of purple silk. By the side of the box place a store of cards and metallic pens that can be used for the children's contributions. Display Kit Wright's poem alongside the box.
● To initiate this ongoing activity, brainstorm the sorts of sights, smells, sounds, textures, animals, dreams, memories, natural phenomenon, and so on that the children may wish to put in the box. Encourage everyone to complete a card to put into it. Ideas can remain anonymous if desired.
● Occasionally, select a number of cards from the box and read out in the same format as the poem. Use the ideas to stimulate constructive discussion. Encourage the children to create new ideas for their magic box whenever you think appropriate.

CAR CAPERS

THINKING SKILL: evaluation
SUBJECT LINK: PSHE
ORGANISATION: whole class
RESOURCES: space to sit in a circle

WHAT TO DO

● The aim of this game is to concentrate on sounds and respond appropriately and with speed.
● Each person is allowed one *screech*, which reverses the play and is indicative of a vehicle spinning round and changing direction.
● To commence, choose a player who makes a *vroom* sound in the direction of their choice.
● The person sitting next to them says *vroom* and so on until someone chooses to use their *screech*. Play then reverses and goes in the other direction.
● Once each child has used their *screech*, the game can stop. The children will be quick to notice if anyone is cheating and trying to use more than one *screech*!

FIZZ BUZZ

THINKING SKILL: information processing
SUBJECT LINK: mathematics
ORGANISATION: whole class
RESOURCES: space to sit in a circle

WHAT TO DO

● Count from zero around the class in numerical order but replace certain numbers with the word fizz or buzz or fizz buzz depending on whether a number falls into the parameters set.
● As a simple example, you may decide to replace any multiples of ten with fizz and any multiples of four with buzz. Play would therefore sound as follows: 0, 1, 2, 3, buzz, 5, 6, 7, buzz, 9, fizz, 11, buzz, 13, 14, 15, buzz, 17, 18, 19, fizz buzz and so on.
● Other ideas would be to replace prime numbers, square roots, square numbers, cube numbers, or any of the times table numbers.
● Should a number be spoken that should have been replaced by fizz or buzz or fizz buzz, that person is out. You will need to adjudicate but you will find that the class will also be eager to point out errors. Play the game with all the children standing up. They sit down when they are out.

TAKE YOUR PLACES!

THINKING SKILL: creative
SUBJECT LINK: literacy
ORGANISATION: whole class
RESOURCES: the register (this activity is particularly useful when you have a visitor to the class)

WHAT TO DO

● As a class, think of as many prepositions as you can and display them on a board. Elicit phrases such as adjacent to; directly behind; to the immediate left of and so on.
● The first person in the register begins with, *Good morning, my name is Jenny Aardvark* [child's name] *and perched on his chair three places to my left is Ryan Brown.* The second person continues with a greeting and proceeds to gesticulate and describe the name and location of the next person in the register. This continues until the register is complete. If someone is absent, the child will note this and continue with the next child in the register. The last person in the register finishes with a greeting such as, *Good morning everybody and welcome to our class.*
● Descriptions of how individuals are sitting or what they are doing may also be incorporated in the introductory greeting – as long as they are complimentary!

TONGUE-TWISTERS

THINKING SKILL: information processing
SUBJECT LINK: literacy
ORGANISATION: whole class
RESOURCES: poetry anthologies containing tongue-twister index cards

WHAT TO DO

● Children can produce tongue-twister index cards and keep them in a box for recitation. The box can be added to over time as and when children come across new tongue-twisters, or record and insert their own.
● Invite individuals to pick a tongue-twister and try it out in front of the class. Other members of the class can then challenge the performance if they think they can improve on it in terms of accuracy and speed.

BULLET POINT BALLOT

THINKING SKILL: reasoning, evaluation
SUBJECT LINK: history, literacy
ORGANISATION: pairs or groups of three, then whole class
RESOURCES: pen and paper or cards; a list of environmental and human rights issues – enough for one issue per group (suggestions may include: cloning to preserve endangered species, developing alternative energy sources, reducing pollution to slow global warming, saving water and so on – these are obviously massive issues but the activity enables the children to develop a cursory understanding and develop their general knowledge.)

WHAT TO DO

● Allocate an issue to each group.
● Explain that only three of these issues are going to be put on the agenda for urgent discussion and action by a World Summit.
● Each group must put forward a case stating why their issue is the most important for the future of the planet. Allow a week for preparation and then hold the debate.
● Each group must present their case verbally and then present a written list of five bullet points setting out their argument.
● Once each case has been heard, hold a ballot.

HISTORICAL WHO AM I?

THINKING SKILL: enquiry
SUBJECT LINK: history
ORGANISATION: individuals and then whole class
RESOURCES: prepare a bank of eight cards and write the name of a famous historical person on each one. You could rely on the children's general knowledge or include four days of preparation time as detailed below. Include a diverse range of people from musicians, politicians, poets, artists, war leaders and so on.

WHAT TO DO

● Allocate a historical figure to each of a group of eight volunteers. Alternatively the volunteers could each pick a card from a 'hat'.
● Each morning and afternoon for four days, two of the volunteers can take turns to give a one- or two-minute speech about the life of the character they have picked, thus providing the class with a bank of knowledge to be tested during the game, which can be played on the fifth day.

● Place the historical figure name cards in a hat and choose a volunteer to pick a card and 'be' that person. The children ask closed questions to establish the person's identity, the historical figure can, thus, only respond with yes or no. The children can opt to take a guess when they think they know who the person is.
● You may like to make a hanging display of the historical figures to remind the children who they are – for example, find a picture of each person, mount it on card and produce a name tag to hang below it.

MENTAL NOUGHTS AND CROSSES

THINKING SKILL: information processing
SUBJECT LINK: mathematics
ORGANISATION: groups of three
RESOURCES: pen and paper

WHAT TO DO

● Choose one player to be the referee. This person has the pen and paper and draws a noughts and crosses grid. Keeping the paper hidden, the referee's job is to record what each player says.
● The two other players decide who is going to be noughts and who is going to be crosses. The aim is the same as for paper noughts and crosses, that is, to complete a line horizontally, vertically or diagonally in either noughts or crosses. The difference, however, is that this game is played mentally. Each player describes where he/she chooses to place his or her mark. For example: *Nought, top left.*

THE BUTCHER'S BISON!

THINKING SKILL: creative
SUBJECT LINK: literacy
ORGANISATION: whole class
RESOURCES: none

WHAT TO DO

● This game is based on 'My Aunt's Cat'. The basic game involves describing 'My Aunt's Cat' with an adjective for each letter of the alphabet.

● For this version of the game, the children should think of a different person, animal and adjective for each letter of the alphabet. For example, *The butcher's bison is a brave bison.* Encourage the children to come up with different jobs or titles or family members rather than names.

● Go around the class, or name someone to start and as they finish their go they nominate the next player. This gives an added element of surprise and anticipation! The class also have to concentrate on who has already had a go.

NAME THE NOUN

THINKING SKILL: creative
SUBJECT LINK: literacy
LEARNING LINK: visual
ORGANISATION: whole class in teams
RESOURCES: timer; word cards – prepare a bank of word cards – you will need at least 30. Each card should have a noun written in bold and two or three other closely associated words beneath it, for example: *Peas - Green/small/round/vegetable.*

WHAT TO DO

● Split the class into four teams, each with a team leader to nominate who is going to be the speaker for each round.

● The first team send their volunteer to the front of the class and he or she has one minute to describe as many of the objects on the cards without saying any of the words that are written

on it. Hand one card to the volunteer at a time. For peas, therefore, it would be permissible to say, *They grow in pods, you eat them with your main course and they are difficult to keep on the fork!*

● The speaker's own team must guess the noun and a referee from another team should challenge if any of the words on the card are used. Each time the group gets a word correct the team scores a point. If an 'illegal' word is used, the other teams all get one point each.

● Once the minute is up, the score is recorded and a volunteer from the second team has a go, and so on.

DOT DASH DOT

THINKING SKILL: information processing
SUBJECT LINK: history
LEARNING LINK: visual
ORGANISATION: pairs
RESOURCES: Morse code alphabet cards; pen and paper

WHAT TO DO

● Provide each child with a Morse code alphabet reference card.

● Demonstrate how to create a short message for the children to record.

● Each child then writes their own message and 'reads' it out for their partner to record and decipher.

MORSE CODE ALPHABET		
A • —	N — •	0 — — — — —
B — • • •	O — — —	1 • — — — —
C — • — •	P • — — •	2 • • — — —
D — • •	Q — — • —	3 • • • — —
E •	R • — •	4 • • • • —
F • • — •	S • • •	5 • • • • •
G — — •	T —	6 — • • • •
H • • • •	U • • —	7 — — • • •
I • •	V • • • —	8 — — — • •
J • — — —	W • — —	9 — — — — •
K — • —	X — • • —	Full stop • — • — • —
L • — • •	Y — • — —	Comma — — • • — —
M — —	Z — — • •	Query • • — — • •

ROUND IT UP

THINKING SKILL: information processing
SUBJECT LINK: mathematics
ORGANISATION: pairs
RESOURCES: calculator; pen and paper; counters

WHAT TO DO

● Players take turns to put a decimal number into the calculator – 18.37, for example.

● Their partner has to say what to add to this number to make it up to the next whole number – 0.63. To avoid disputes, the sum is recorded on a piece of paper, which has been divided into two columns – one column for each player.

● The first player adds the suggestion to the number on the calculator and if it is correct, a counter is awarded to the player who gave the answer. Play then swaps.

● Continue for a set length of time or for an agreed number of rounds. Play may become quite difficult if players realise that they can insert numbers such as 12.000457!

LISTEN AND LEARN

THINKING SKILL: evaluation
SUBJECT LINK: PSHE, citizenship
ORGANISATION: pairs with someone they do not really know, and whole class
RESOURCES: stopwatch

WHAT TO DO

● The children decide who is A and who is B. A is going to speak first while B listens.

● A should talk about him/herself for 1 minute, giving details of family, hobbies, views, opinions, aspirations and so on.

● When the minute is up, B reports back to A what he/she has learned. This will be reported in the second person. For example,

You have three brothers and sisters, your most memorable day was when you flew in a hot air balloon…

● Swap roles so that everyone experiences speaking and listening to their partner. At the end, randomly select individuals to report to the class what they have learned about their partner. This will obviously be reported in the third person. Ask a few speakers to report to the class on how well their partner listened.

● This can be used as an exercise in demonstrating the use of the first, second and third person.

YOUR MINUTE STARTS NOW…

THINKING SKILL: reasoning, creative
SUBJECT LINK: literacy – speaking and listening
ORGANISATION: whole class
RESOURCES: stopwatch; list of subjects

WHAT TO DO

● Write up a list of subjects on the board. Some ideas might be:

The best day of my life.
A hot air balloon ride.
My views on homework.
My views on waste.

● Ask for volunteers and select four or five for the session.

● Volunteers take turns to speak for a whole minute on one of the subjects listed. They are given 20 points to start with. Points are deducted from this score if a valid challenge is made by another child while they are speaking. Challenges can be made for hesitation, repetition and digression. An incorrect or unfair challenge results in an extra point being awarded to the speaker. Stop the clock if a challenge is made.

● At the end of the session, the winner is the child with the most points. Keep a record of who has volunteered and encourage other children to be speakers on different occasions.

THE FURNITURE GAME

THINKING SKILL: reasoning/creative
SUBJECT LINK: literacy – speaking and listening
ORGANISATION: whole class
RESOURCES: list of famous people or characters from books familiar to the class

WHAT TO DO

● This game is a useful tool for developing the ability to think in an abstract manner. Be wary of using people in the class as your subjects, unless you can be certain that everyone can be relied upon to play the game in a sensitive manner.

● First ask the class to think of a list of categories – food, furniture, seasons, weather, cars, sports, clothes, animals, environment and so on. Write up on the board.

● Choose a person or character whose personality is well known to all to demonstrate how to play the game. Discuss the person's personality – are they jolly, cheerful, kind, cruel?

● Next ask the children, If this person was a piece of furniture, what would they be? Explain that someone who is warm and cuddly, might be likened to a comfy armchair; someone who is full of good ideas and enthusiasm might be like a refreshing shower.

● Once you have created a metaphorical image of the person using several different examples, and you are happy that the class understands the concept, invite a volunteer to choose a character (either from a list or of their own choice). The class then take turns to ask the person to describe their character according to different categories.

WHEN I WENT ON SAFARI, I…

THINKING SKILL: information processing, creativity
SUBJECT LINK: literacy – speaking and listening
ORGANISATION: whole class or split into two groups
RESOURCES: a small soft ball or beanbag

WHAT TO DO

● The well-known game 'When I went on holiday…' can be used to develop memory and language skills. To vary the game and encourage creativity, use the following prompts as alternatives:

When I went on safari I saw …
When I was stranded on a desert island I took with me …
When I made a picnic for aliens I packed …

● Sit in a circle with one child holding the ball. Only the child holding the ball should speak. The first person begins building a 'list' by reciting the starter sentence and completing it with their suggestion. Encourage the children to create an adjectival phrase rather than just suggesting a noun. For example, *When I went on safari I saw a purple, custard-eating elephant…*

● The first person then throws the ball to the person they wish to go next. This person recites the sentence and adds on his or her own suggestion. For example, *When I went on safari I saw a purple, custard eating elephant and a tiger in a tutu!* Play continues until everyone has had a go. The aim is to try to get everyone to make a contribution and to be able to recite the whole list.

LANGUAGE BINGO

THINKING SKILL: information processing
SUBJECT LINK: modern languages
LEARNING LINK: visual
ORGANISATION: whole class
RESOURCES: paper and pen and/or counters; word cards (see below) in a box; a piece of paper divided into nine squares (three by three); a pen for each child (this is the simplest and quickest way to resource this game – alternatively, prepare bingo cards and use counters)

WHAT TO DO

● On the board, write up between 20 and 30 words in French, Spanish or another modern language – the words should be ones the children have been learning or are familiar with.

● The children select nine of these words and write one in each square. Ask them to hold their cards up once they have completed this (to check for cheats!)

● Write the English equivalent of each of the words you have written up on the board, onto small cards. Place these in a bag or box.

● Select a caller and play language bingo. The winner is the first player to cross off all the words on their card. Check that the winner has correctly translated all the words. You will need to keep the cards that have been called out separate, for reference. This is a great way to learn foreign vocabulary!

CAN YOU WRITE IT?

THINKING SKILL: information processing
SUBJECT LINK: history, any
LEARNING LINK: visual
ORGANISATION: individuals (pair the children sensitively for marking purposes)
RESOURCES: pen and paper; dictation passage (see below)

WHAT TO DO

● Read out the following passage for dictation.

> *The Ancient Greek Olympics*
> *The Olympic Games began in Olympia in Ancient Greece in approximately 776 BC. The Greeks believed that athletic skills were the gifts of the gods.*
> *To begin with, the only event was a running race. Later on, however, boxing, wrestling, the pentathlon and horse and chariot racing were included.*
> *The sprint remained the most important event. It was held over a distance of 192 metres, which was said to be the distance that Hercules could run in just one breath! It was Hercules who was the mythical founder of the games.*

● The objective of the dictation should be clearly stated as being spelling, punctuation or possibly both.
● Carry out the dictation and then ask the children to swap books. Write up the passage slowly, stopping to point out difficult spellings and punctuation.
● The children can use scoring to quantify how their partner has performed. Allocate a starting number of points from which points are deducted for errors.

WORD ASSOCIATION

THINKING SKILL: creative
SUBJECT LINK: literacy – speaking and listening
ORGANISATION: whole class
RESOURCES: none

WHAT TO DO

● When taking the register, begin with a word for word association. Each child responds to their name with the first word that comes into their mind, associated with the preceding word (the one the previous child has used).

● If a word has already been said, the class can call out repetition and that person has to think of another word.
● Record the starting and finishing words to see where the word association led.

DESERT ISLAND SURVIVAL

THINKING SKILL: reasoning
SUBJECT LINK: literacy
ORGANISATION: six groups (approximately)
RESOURCES: none

WHAT TO DO

● Ask the children to imagine that they have been stranded on a desert island. Discuss human 'needs' and establish a number of 'needs' categories – these may include: food, water, shelter, clothing, entertainment, comforts, mental stimulation and so on.
● Each group has to discuss and nominate a single item that they would take with them for each category. They have to be able to validate their choice and explain how it would meet their needs.
● Draw up a table on the board with categories down the side and group names along the top. The group leaders should come up and write in their suggestions. Debate the suggestions and then take a vote on each category (groups are not allowed to vote for their own suggestions!)
● Finally, make a list of the ultimate Class Desert Island Survival Kit.

NOW TRY THIS

Decide on a number of obvious items that are to be disallowed, such as a knife, gun, and rope. This is to make the activity more challenging.

FUTURE FORTUNES

THINKING SKILL: enquiry, creative
SUBJECT LINK: literacy
ORGANISATION: groups or individual
RESOURCES: a 'crystal ball'; black cloth; magic wand and so on; strips of paper and pens

WHAT TO DO

● Set the scene to create an imaginative atmosphere.
● Create an image of a mysterious fortune-teller who has a crystal ball with which he/she can see into the future.
● Tell the children that they are allowed to ask the fortune-teller six questions – two about themselves, two about their family and friends, and two about the world.
● Share and compare the questions and hold a discussion about the implications of knowing about the future and what they might not want to know and why.

GUESS THE OBJECT

THINKING SKILL: enquiry
SUBJECT LINK: science
ORGANISATION: groups or whole class
RESOURCES: paper and pencil

WHAT TO DO

● This game is an old favourite but is useful for developing the skill of asking relevant questions. It also helps the children to learn the difference between closed and open questions. Think of an object which is an 'animal', 'mineral' or 'vegetable' and write it secretly on a piece of paper.
● The class then ask 20 closed questions (keep a tally) to try to determine what the object is.
● If the object is guessed correctly before the 20 questions have been asked the class win, if not, the player wins. Remind the children to be wary of making too many 'wild' guesses as these count as questions!
● The person to guess correctly thinks of the next object.

TIME TO GO

THINKING SKILL: information processing
SUBJECT LINK: mathematics
ORGANISATION: individual
RESOURCES: none - an activity for leaving the class in an orderly fashion

WHAT TO DO

● Use the 24-hour clock. Choose a character. Begin with a time – say 20:30 – and describe an activity that takes a certain amount of time.
● The children work out the time the activity is completed and put their hand up – select a child to answer. If the time they suggest is correct they may line up.
● Continue describing activities until everyone has had a turn.

Some examples:
Start time 20:30. Billy sleeps for 9 hours until the cockerel next door crows and wakes him up. (05:30)
He looks at his clock, rolls over and goes back to sleep for 1¼ hours. (06:45)
The alarm goes off and he jumps out of bed and has a wash, which takes 15 minutes. (07:00)
He throws his school things in a bag and stumbles downstairs – this takes 12 minutes. (07:12)
He eats toast and drinks a glass of milk which takes 4 minutes. (07:16)
He writes a quick essay about the reign of Queen Victoria, which takes him until 07:30. (14 minutes)
Then he rushes out the door and runs down the road to catch the school bus. This takes him 17 minutes. (07:47)
The bus leaves at 08:00 so he has to wait (13 minutes).

RIDDLE TIME

THINKING SKILL: information processing
SUBJECT LINK: literacy
ORGANISATION: individual
RESOURCES: riddles

WHAT TO DO

● Ask the children to solve the following riddles:

> *What is it that the more you take away the larger it becomes?*
>
> *What holds water yet is full of holes?*
>
> *What is it that you will break even when you name it?*
>
> *What belongs to you but others use it more than you do?*
>
> *The more you take, the more you leave behind. What are they?*
>
> *What comes once in a minute, twice in a moment, but never in a hundred years?*

ANSWERS
A hole; a sponge; silence; your name; footsteps; the letter 'm'

NOW TRY THIS

Challenge the children to make up their own riddles for the following words: an onion, a shadow, a towel, and a cold.

PERFORMANCE POETRY

THINKING SKILL: creative
SUBJECT LINK: literacy
ORGANISATION: groups
RESOURCES: recording facility; www.bbc.co.uk/arts/poetry/outloud; poetry anthologies.

WHAT TO DO

● Go to the above website and listen to a range of poets performing their own work – Roger McGough, Benjamin Zephaniah, Sir John Betjemen and more. Select examples suitable for Key Stage 2 children.
● Listen to the poems together. Discuss how the poets performed their works and how effective the performance was.
● Select a poem for each group to perform. *The Works* chosen by Paul Cookson has a section on performance poetry. Each group should discuss how to perform the poem effectively, practise and then record their poem.
● Play all the poems to the whole class to listen to. Children can constructively comment on the performances they hear.

WHAT DO YOU THINK?

THINKING SKILL: evaluation
SUBJECT LINK: citizenship, PSHE
ORGANISATION: group and whole class
RESOURCES: attitude statements on board

WHAT TO DO

● Ask the children what they think is meant by the term attitude.
● Discuss the implications of the following statements and come up with examples of what they could mean.
  ● Attitude is as important as ability when it comes to your success.
  ● Life is full of choices – make sure you choose carefully.
  ● You are responsible for your own actions.
  ● Self-control is knowing you can – but deciding you won't.
  ● Courage means not being afraid to do the right thing.
  ● To think we need to have an open mind.

ANTI-SMOKING RAP

THINKING SKILL: creative
SUBJECT LINK: PSHE
ORGANISATION: groups
RESOURCES: recording facilities; microphone; paper and pens

WHAT TO DO

● Hold a discussion about smoking.
● Create a thought map of all the key words that arise from the discussion.
● Use these to create an anti-smoking rap. Refine, practise and perform.
● Finally, record the raps.

AGONY AUNT

THINKING SKILL: reasoning
SUBJECT LINK: citizenship
ORGANISATION: small groups
RESOURCES: agony aunt letters – one for each group (some examples are given below but you may want to create your own. This may be a useful opportunity to deal with current issues.)

WHAT TO DO

● Each group is to act as a panel of agony aunt writers (explain what an agony aunt is) for a young person's magazine.
● Read out one of the problem letters that the magazine has received.
● Each group should discuss how the magazine is going to respond to them.

> *Dear Agony Aunt,*
> *Please help me. I am 11 years old and my group of friends has started smoking in the park after school before the bus collects us. They all think they are really cool but I hate it. It makes me feel sick and I know that it is addictive and I know that my mum would kill me if she knew. What should I do?*

> *Dear Agony Aunt,*
> *I have been invited to my friend's brother's 16th birthday party. I am only 12 but everyone says I look a lot older. I know they are planning to have alcoholic drinks – I don't want to spoil my friend's fun by not joining in but I'm scared of the effects of alcohol. What advice can you give me?*

SCHOOL SOUND QUIZ

THINKING SKILL: enquiry
SUBJECT LINK: speaking and listening
LEARNING LINK: kinaesthetic
ORGANISATION: groups of four or five children, whole class follow up
RESOURCES: tape recorder with microphone and blank tape; pen and paper

WHAT TO DO

● Ask the children to go around the school in small groups (one group at a time), listening for familiar and unusual sounds.
● After touring the school, each group should decide on ten sounds to record for a quiz. Choose a group name and make a recorded introduction to the quiz before beginning the recording. When recording each sound, they should introduce each one with a number so that the sounds can easily be distinguished from each other.
● Once all the quizzes have been recorded, try them out in class. Were some sounds recorded by more than one group? How easy were the sounds to identify? Which group was the champion sound detective?

HOT SEAT

THINKING SKILL: enquiry
SUBJECT LINK: geography
ORGANISATION: whole class, individuals for the 'Hot Seat'
RESOURCES: a video or radio recording of an interview with someone who has survived a disaster (the interview with Tsunami Victim Ari Afrizal, who survived 15 days at sea on a raft is a good example, www.bbc.co.uk/news provides video and auditory footage of archived news articles); alternatively a copy of a written interview; chair and carpet space; question strips

WHAT TO DO

● View, listen or read the chosen interview through together. Explain that the children can have thinking time until the next day to prepare one or more questions for the person on the hot seat.
● Provide them with question strips for recording their questions. Ensure that they prepare open questions (*What did it feel like when... What will you do now that...?*) Explain that closed questions result in a yes/no response and that this would result in an uninteresting 'Hot Seat' session.
● Ask for a volunteer to act as the person featured in the interview. The volunteer will take on the identity of this person and respond to questions as if he/she is that person. He/she will need to use the thinking time to re-read the interview and develop empathy with the person and his/her experiences.
● Carry out the 'Hot Seat' interview with the volunteer sitting on the chair and the rest of the class sitting comfortably around him/her. Creating a relaxed atmosphere is important for this type of activity.

TIMES IT

THINKING SKILL: information processing
SUBJECT LINK: mathematics
LEARNING LINK: visual
ORGANISATION: pairs – of similar ability in mathematics
RESOURCES: four sets of number cards 0–12 (for each pair); pen and paper; table chart (for checking)

WHAT TO DO

● The children shuffle the cards and deal them face down between the two players.
● Simultaneously, they turn over the top card and multiply the two numbers shown on the cards.
● The first player to call out the correct answer scores a point. Record the points scored under two columns using tallies. Continue play as long as you wish.

WEATHER WATCH

THINKING SKILL: reasoning
SUBJECT LINK: geography
ORGANISATION: groups
RESOURCES: large sheets of paper and pens

WHAT TO DO

● Talk about the weather! On the board, make a list of all the different types of weather you can think of (you may want to restrict the activity to weather in the UK). Ask the children which types of weather generally occur in which season?
● Discuss how the weather can impact on our daily lives.

NOW TRY THIS

Extend each idea with further branches:

> fog – traffic queues – people being late – causing stress – accidents –arguments
>
> Freezing temperatures – need more heating – higher fuel bills – old people worry – illness

BULLYING BRAINSTORM

THINKING SKILL: reasoning/enquiry
SUBJECT LINK: citizenship/PSHE
ORGANISATION: groups, then whole class
RESOURCES: large sheets of paper and marker pens; board

WHAT TO DO

● Write the following questions on large sheets of paper, one sheet for each group and each question in its own thought bubble.
> What is bullying?
> Why do people bully other people?
> What can you do if you see someone being bullied?
> What can you do when someone is bullying you?
● Ask what they think will happen if an adult is told. Instruct each group to discuss and write their answers as branches from each cloud.
● Follow the session up by reviewing the school policy on bullying in the light of the ideas they have discussed.

TARGET TAPES

THINKING SKILL: evaluation
SUBJECT LINK: PSHE
ORGANISATION: individual
RESOURCES: tape recorder with microphone; blank tape

WHAT TO DO

● Carry out this activity at the beginning of a term or half term.
● Everybody decides on a realistic target to aim for by the end of the term or half-term. This may be a general target such as remembering to bring in homework on time, or improving handwriting, or checking work before handing it in. Alternatively, the target may be subject-specific related to an achievement in a certain area such as learning how to carry out long division.
● Once the targets have been decided, the class should record them on tape. Write the general dialogue on the board and then the children can fill in the details on an individual basis. For example:

> My name is Jonathon Gregory and this term I am going to try my best to underline my titles and dates and write in a neat cursive style.

• Once everybody has recorded their target – including the teacher – store the tape somewhere handy. Bring it out and play it at intervals during the term, as a reminder of what everybody is setting out to achieve.

• At the end of the term, listen to the recording again and decide whether the targets were achieved, whether progress was made or whether the target still needs working on. Make a new recording stating the conclusions that were reached as a celebration of effort. For example:

> *My name is Jonathan Gregory and this term I have really tried hard to underline my work and I am writing in a cursive style. I am really proud of what I have achieved. Next term I will try to write neatly ALL the time!*

TIME CAPSULE

THINKING SKILL: reasoning
SUBJECT LINK: history
LEARNING LINK: tactile
ORGANISATION: individual
RESOURCES: pen and paper

WHAT TO DO

• Ask the class to decide on five objects to bury in a time capsule to give a picture of life at the start of the 21st century.

• They should accompany each item with a recorded verbal statement describing the object and its relevance and importance on either a personal or general level. Providing categories will structure the activity. Suggestions include toys, work, school, clothing, films, transport, communication, food, furniture, music, and politics.

• Share the children's decisions with the whole class.

• Make the time capsules and put in digital photos of the objects and the accompanying recordings made by the children.

CINEMA SEATING

THINKING SKILL: information processing
SUBJECT LINK: mathematics
LEARNING LINK: visual
ORGANISATION: individual
RESOURCES: cinema plan for each child; seating description; pencils

WHAT TO DO

• Ask the children to listen as you read out the description of the seating arrangements below.

• They then use the information to complete the cinema seating-plan and discover which is the only seat to remain empty (5A).

Seating instructions

	Projection Room	Toilets		Exit	
	Sophie	Su	Linda	Neela	Holly	D
Fire Exit	Harry	Cameron	Barney	Lucie	Becky	C
	Yan	Ollie	Sienna	George	Sam	B
Ice Cream Lady	Carl	Charlie	Ryan	Rosie	X	A
	1	2	3	4	5	

Screen

• Holly sits closest to the exit.
• Neela sits on her right.
• Harry sits closest to the fire exit. In front of him is Yan, behind him is Sophie.
• Next to Sophie is Su.
• Linda sits nearest to the toilet.
• Carl will be first in the queue for ice cream and lollies.
• Charlie and Ryan have front row seats.
• Su sits three rows behind Charlie and Linda sits three rows behind Ryan.
• Barney and Sienna sit in the middle of the cinema. Barney is in line with the fire exit.
• Ollie sits between Sienna and Yan.
• Becky sits in 5C. To her right is Lucie.
• Sam and George sit in row B.
• Sam only has one person sitting next to him.
• Cameron sits in row C.
• Rosie occupies a front row seat.

BOOK AUCTION

THINKING SKILL: reasoning
SUBJECT LINK: literacy
ORGANISATION: individual in front of whole class
RESOURCES: fiction books; tokens

WHAT TO DO

● Explain how an auction works. Allocate a set number of tokens to each child – alternatively the children could 'earn' their tokens through the week preceding the auction – the harder they work the more tokens they earn!

● Keep a record of how many tokens the children have earned and then award them their tokens on the day of the auction.

● Choose about ten auctioneers whose job it will be to select a fiction book that they have personally read and enjoyed.

● The auctioneers prepare a sales blurb for their chosen book in order to try to sell it to the highest bidder.

● The class listens to the sales blurbs for each book. Individuals can then bid for the book they would like to read, using their tokens. The highest bidder can borrow the book to read first.

CONSEQUENCE CHAINS

THINKING SKILL: enquiry
SUBJECT LINK: citizenship
ORGANISATION: groups
RESOURCES: board; large sheets of paper; pens

WHAT TO DO

● Split the class into four groups. Explain what a consequence is. Pose the obvious question; *What would you do if you won the lottery…?*

● After the initial 'imaginary spending spree' take one of the ideas and develop it further – demonstrating the consequences of each action.

● Record the responses as a chain of events – an arrow joining one consequence to the next.

● Brainstorm a list of 'What if…?' questions. For example: 'What if the world ran out of oil?' 'What if you could become invisible?' For each round, select a 'What if…?' question. The challenge is to create the longest chain of consequences leading from the initial dilemma.

WHAT'S MY NUMBER?

THINKING SKILL: enquiry
SUBJECT LINK: mathematics
ORGANISATION: individual and whole class
RESOURCES: none

WHAT TO DO

● Discuss how a number could be classified by using the following terms: factor, multiples, prime numbers, odd, even and so on.

● Choose a volunteer to think of a number. The class is allowed ten closed questions to try to guess the value of the number. The volunteer can, therefore, only answer yes or no to the questions.

● If the class do not guess after ten questions the volunteer can opt to choose another number or delegate to another class member.

MNEMONICS

THINKING SKILL: creative
SUBJECT LINK: literacy
LEARNING LINK: visual
ORGANISATION: groups of three or four
RESOURCES: whiteboards and pens; cards for each letter

WHAT TO DO:

● Choose a list of words that are difficult to spell.

● Allocate a word to each group.

● Each group will need sufficient cards for each letter in the word.

- Devise a mnemonic for each word and use a card for each letter and its associated word –demonstrate the mnemonic by holding up and reading out the cards.
- Store the cards so that the children can arrange them into the correct order and check the spelling.

ROOM 101

THINKING SKILL: creative
SUBJECT LINK: PSHE
LEARNING LINK: tactile
ORGANISATION: whole class
RESOURCES: none

WHAT TO DO

- Discuss the concept of Room 101, which was the room in George Orwell's book *1984*, which contained 'the worst thing in the world'. Once banished there, he/she or it could never be retrieved.
- Everyone should think of something to send to Room 101 and prepare to be challenged about this decision. Invite suggestions and challenges and then take a class vote to decide which items will actually be banished to Room 101.
- Make a small Room 101 display and add items to the list as each person's ideas are discussed.

WHAT GOES AROUND…

THINKING SKILL: enquiry
SUBJECT LINK: science
ORGANISATION: pairs
RESOURCES: glass of water; paper; pens; timeline

WHAT TO DO

- Introduce the activity by showing the class the glass of water and telling them that roughly the same amount of water has been on Earth since the days when dinosaurs roamed the land. This means that the water in the glass in front of them is as old as the Earth!
- Show the children a timeline, picking out different periods to stimulate thinking. In pairs, ask them to try to think of lots of questions about where the glass of water may have been or what or who it may have been part of. The children will inevitably link urination with this idea! To avoid silliness, explain that this is obviously part of the recycling system and explain ways in which water is purified.
- The discussions that could arise from this activity are endless – water shortages, illness caused by drinking dirty water and so on.

ALPHABET CATEGORIES

THINKING SKILL: creative
SUBJECT LINK: all
LEARNING LINK: visual
ORGANISATION: groups
RESOURCES: pen and paper; dictionaries; atlases; stopwatch; the letters of the alphabet on individual cards stored in a container; a list of categories (decide upon these with the class) written on cards stored in a second container (examples may include countries, cities, vegetables, girls' names, boys' names, animals, flowers, birds, rivers, and words of four syllables)

WHAT TO DO

- Someone picks a letter and a category from each container. The groups then have a set time to list as many things from the chosen category beginning with the chosen letter.
- When the time is up they submit their answers to the 'judge' and get one point for each correct answer. Allocate a bonus point to groups who think of ideas that no one else has thought of.

TANGRAMS

THINKING SKILL: creative
SUBJECT LINK: mathematics
LEARNING LINK: visual
ORGANISATION: individual
RESOURCES: squared paper or card; scissors

WHAT TO DO:

● Ask the children to do the following:

● Make the shape below out of piece of square card. It is helpful if you divide the square into four by four squares.

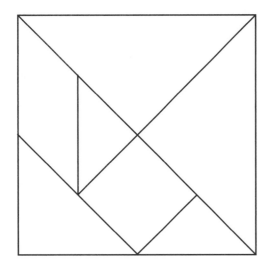

● Cut along the lines to make seven separate pieces. There should be two small triangles, one medium triangle, two large triangles, one square and one parallelogram.

● The seven-piece puzzle is called a tangram – an ancient puzzle from China. Hundreds of different pictures can be made from the pieces but there are some simple rules:

   ● You must use all seven pieces.

   ● Each piece must touch another piece but not overlap it.

● Try to create the following images using your set of tangram pieces:

   dog
   cat
   shark
   swan

ANSWERS

dog

cat

shark

swan

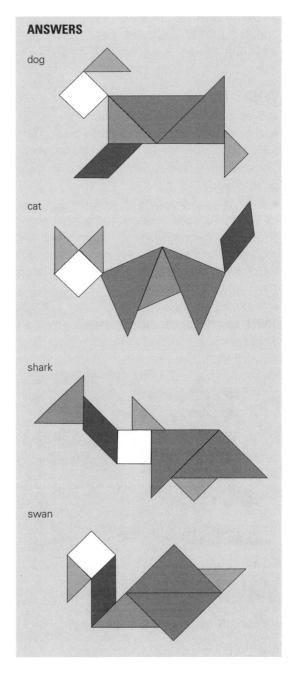

NOW TRY THIS

There are hundreds more patterns that can be created using tangrams. Ask the children to use 'tangram' as a key word for a search on the internet to locate further puzzles to try out.

MATCHING TIME

THINKING SKILL: information processing
SUBJECT LINK: mathematics
LEARNING LINK: visual
ORGANISATION: pairs
RESOURCES: A4 card in two colours; a stopwatch

WHAT TO DO

● Divide a sheet of A4 paper into 8 rectangles – in each rectangle write the following time periods:

　a. 12:50am – 01:40am
　b. 01:00am– 6:30pm
　c. 3:59pm – 6:34pm
　d. 11:56pm – 3:47am
　e. 4:00pm to 7:32pm
　f. 12:30am – 12:40pm
　g. 8:32am – 10: 48am
　h. 10:45am – 3:20pm

● On a second sheet of A4 paper again divided into eight rectangles write the following times:

　1. 3 hours 51 minutes
　2. 3 hours 32 minutes
　3. 50 minutes
　4. 2 hours 35 minutes
　5. 2 hours 16 minutes
　6. 17 hours 30 minutes
　7. 4 hours 35 minutes
　8. 12 hours 10 minutes

● Photocopy the time periods onto one colour of card and the times onto a different coloured card. You need to copy one set of cards for each pair. Cut the rectangles into separate cards.

● Give each pair a set of the 16 cards, to spread out on their desk.

● Start the clock. The winning pair is the first to correctly match the time elapsed to the correct time period.

● As a pair finishes give them their time. They can then check their answers against an answer sheet. In this way, everyone gets to complete the activity and check their own answers.

ANSWERS					
a/3	b/6	c /4	d/1	e/2	f/8
g/5	h/7				

NOW TRY THIS

1. The children make different sets of cards to use to challenge their friends. How fast can different sets be matched?
2. Try making matching sets for other subjects, such as matching words between different languages.

MAKE A MAGRITTE

THINKING SKILL: creative
SUBJECT LINK: art
LEARNING LINK: visual
ORGANISATION: individual
RESOURCES: old magazines, catalogues, leaflets and so on; scissors; glue; sugar paper.

WHAT TO DO

● Introduce the children to the painter René Magritte.

> *Magritte was a surrealist painter who lived and worked in Belgium. Surrealism was a type of art that started in the 1920's in France and spread all over Europe. Surrealist painters tried to make their paintings look really unusual. They painted pictures from their imagination and their memories – Magritte painted ordinary objects in strange places. He changed the size of things and changed parts of things. He also changed the texture of things.*

● View Magritte's work on the internet. Useful art websites include www.artchive.com. Suggested examples of his work suitable for study with Year 5/6 include *L'aimable vérité, A Little of the Bandits' Soul, Le sihcle de lumihres, La Grande famille.*

● Having discussed the paintings, ask the children to carefully cut out images of people and everyday objects from the collection of magazines and catalogues. They can stick these onto contrasting backgrounds, or create their own backgrounds.

● They can then stick their own Magritte-inspired creations onto sugar paper for display.

NOW TRY THIS

Encourage the children to create imaginative titles for their work.

MIXED UP MONARCHS!

THINKING SKILL: enquiry and information processing

SUBJECT LINK: history

LEARNING LINK: visual

ORGANISATION: individual

RESOURCES: eight small boxes labelled with the names of the following English royal houses: Saxons (1042–1066), Plantagenets (1154–1399), House of Lancaster (1399–1461), House of York (1461–1485), Tudors (1485–1603), Stuarts (1603–1649), House of Hanover (1714–1901), Windsor (1910–present day); sticky labels; English monarch cards (name and dates) cut up and mixed-up in a bag (the children can research and make up cards for the remaining periods – House of Wessex (802–1016), Danish (1014–1042), Normans (1066–1154), Commonwealth (1649–1659), Stuarts (restored) (1659–1714), Saxe-Coburg-Gotha (1901–1910) if there is time.)

Saxons	
Edward (the Confessor)	1042–1066
Harold II	1066
Plantagenets	
Henry II	1154–1189
Richard I	1189–1199
John	1199–1216
Henry III	1216–1272
Edward I	1272–1307
Edward II	1307–1327
Edward III	1327–1377
Richard II	1377–1399
House of Lancaster	
Henry IV	1399–1413
Henry V	1413–1422
Henry VI	1422–1461
House of York	
Edward IV	1461–1483
Edward V	1483
Richard III	1483–1485
Tudors	
Henry VI	1485–1509
Henry VIII	1509–1547
Edward VI	1547–1553
Jane Grey	1553
Mary I	1553–1558
Elizabeth I	1558–1603
Stuarts	
James I	1603–1625
Charles I	1625–1649

House of Hanover	
George I	1714–1727
George II	1727–1760
George III	1760–1820
George IV	1820–1830
William IV	1830–1837
Victoria	1837–1901
House of Windsor	
George V	1910–1936
Edward VIII	1936–1936
George VI	1936–1952
Elizabeth II	1952–present

WHAT TO DO

● Introduce the concept of a monarchy to the class, explaining that it is the oldest form of government in the United Kingdom. An excellent overview of the history of the English crown can be found at www.royal.gov.uk. Explain that the kings and queens who ruled fell into different historic periods. Each box represents a different period.

● Sort the monarch cards into the correct boxes. When all the cards have been sorted, complete a chronological list.

CREATIVE CURVES

THINKING SKILL: information processing and creative

SUBJECT LINK: mathematics

LEARNING LINK: visual

ORGANISATION: individual

RESOURCES: graph or squared paper; fine felt tips or sharp coloured pencils; rulers

WHAT TO DO

● Ask the children to draw a vertical line and a horizontal line so that they create a cross. The point where they cross is zero and the axes are numbered outwards from this point. They should number the axes from 0 to 10 in each direction.

● In each quarter of the cross, the children join the co-ordinates that add up to 11, that is (1,10), (2,9), (3,8) etc.

● Ask them to carry this out in all four quarters to create an effective pattern.

NOW TRY THIS

Try using different colours in different ways to create different effects.

RANGOLI PATTERNS

THINKING SKILL: creative
SUBJECT LINK: RE
LEARNING LINK: visual
ORGANISATION: groups
RESOURCES: coloured chalks; examples of Rangoli patterns from books or the internet

WHAT TO DO

● The Hindu festival of Divali celebrates the victory of good over evil, light over darkness and it is a time to make a fresh start. Divali literally means 'a row of lights'. At Divali, Hindus put lights at their windows and decorate their doorsteps with Rangoli patterns. Women traditionally make Rangoli patterns, using coloured ground rice limestone or ground chalk, which is arranged in detailed patterns.

● Study examples of Rangoli patterns with the children and then invite them to create examples on a paved area outside the classroom. Encourage children to find out more about the festival of Divali and recount what they have found out in order to develop a deeper understanding of the Hindu faith. Any Hindu children in the class could be invited to give a talk.

PASS THE RING

THINKING SKILL: enquiry
SUBJECT LINK: PSHE
LEARNING LINK: visual
ORGANISATION: whole class
RESOURCES: a long piece of string; a ring

WHAT TO DO

● Thread a ring onto a long piece of string and tie the ends together.

● Ask the class to stand in a circle with both hands holding the string. One member of the class holds the ring in his or her hand so that it cannot be seen.

● A volunteer stands in the centre of the circle and observes the faces and hands of the rest of the class.

● The string is then passed through the children's hands, passing the ring at the same time.

● The volunteer at the centre has to tap the hand of the person he/she thinks has the ring after careful observation.

● If the person concealing the ring is discovered they swap places with the volunteer, if not, the volunteer has to stay in the middle. This is an excellent team builder activity.

FIBONACCI FOLLOW-ON

THINKING SKILL: reasoning
SUBJECT LINK: mathematics
LEARNING LINK: visual
ORGANISATION: individual
RESOURCES: pen and paper; flower identification books; flowers (with all petals in tact)

WHAT TO DO

● The Fibonacci sequence refers to a simple number pattern which can be found everywhere in nature, named after Leonardo of Pisa, a mathematician born in Pisa in about 1175 AD. He was one of the first people to introduce the Hindu–Arabic number system into Europe – the positional system we use today based on ten digits with its decimal point and a symbol for zero: 1 2 3 4 5 6 7 8 9 0.

● In this sequence the last two numbers are added together to give the next number:

0+1=1	1+1=2	2+1=3	2+3=5	3+5=8
1	1	2	3	5

● Ask the children to calculate the next five numbers in the sequence.

● Explore Fibonacci sequences in nature – pine cones, daisies, sunflowers and palm trees all show Fibonacci numbers. For example, pineapples have eight seeds arranged in a clockwise spiral and 13 in an anticlockwise spiral. The arrangement of leaves around a stem also involves Fibonacci numbers.

● Investigate petal patterns in flowers. They should tabulate their results using three columns – name of flower, number of petals and Fibonacci number – Yes /No.

ORIGAMI BOX

THINKING SKILL: information processing, creative
SUBJECT LINK: art, mathematics
LEARNING LINK: auditory
ORGANISATION: pairs
RESOURCES: two 20cm by 20cm squares of thin coloured card for each child; a set of instructions for making an origami box and lid for each pair

WHAT TO DO

● In pairs, the children decide who is going to read out and interpret the instructions and who is going to construct the box. These roles should then be reversed for making the lid.

● When the children have finished, display the results and hold a discussion about how they found the exercise – both in terms of interpreting instructions and working as a pair.

1. Fold a sheet of paper in half and then open it up again. Fold each side edge (parallel to the crease) to meet in the centre (as shown).
2. Fold the edges in the centre back by 1cm. Then fold them back to their original position.
3. Fold the outer corners to the crease of the previous (1cm) fold.
4. Fold back the (1cm) flaps over the corners.
5. Fold the bottom and top parts of the shape as indicated (the crease should be along the edge of the corner that has been folded over). Return them back again.
6. Put your thumbs behind the flaps and pull them back to form the box.
Pinch the corners edges of the box to make it stand up

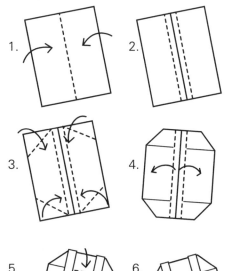

SPIROLATERALS

THINKING SKILL: information processing
SUBJECT LINK: mathematics, art
LEARNING LINK: visual
ORGANISATION: individual
RESOURCES: ruler; pencils and colouring pencils; squared paper

WHAT TO DO

● Start to create a table for the times tables up to 12. The children can copy it and complete it. It should be an extended version of the following:

2-times table	Digit addition	3-times table	Digit addition
1×2=2	2	3	3
2×2=4	4	6	6
3×2=6	6	9	9
4×2=8	8	12	3
5×2=10	1+0=1	15	6
6×2=12	1+2=3	18	9
7×2=14	1+4=5	21	3
8×2=16	1+6=7	24	6
9×2=18	1+8=9	27	9
10×2=20	2+0=2	30	3
11×2=22	2+2=4	33	6
12×2=24	2+4=6	36	9

● In the column headed 'Digit addition', the sum of the digits in the times table column to the left has been added until a single digit is achieved.

● Once this has been completed, discuss the patterns that have emerged.

● Ask the children to choose one of the tables and on squared paper, draw a line the length of the first number. For example, for the 3-times table, draw a line 3cm long. Now turn the page 90 degrees to the right (or left – but turn it the same way each time!) and draw a line 6cm long from the end point of the first line. Then turn the page 90 degrees to the right again and draw a line 9cm long. Continue doing this until you return to the beginning of your pattern and your lines are retracing themselves.

● The children can then decorate the patterns that emerge.

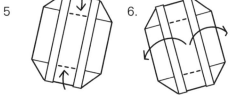

STICKY PROBLEMS

THINKING SKILL: reasoning
SUBJECT LINK: mathematics
LEARNING LINK: visual
ORGANISATION: pairs or small groups
RESOURCES: 20 matches or straws or similar 'sticks' for each pair; a counter for each pair.

WHAT TO DO

● Draw the arrangements for each problem on the board and write the instructions beneath them.
● The children recreate the arrangements on the board using the sticks and try to solve the following puzzles:

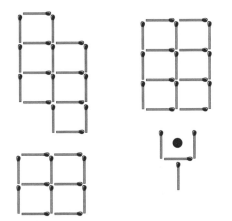

● Remove two matches so that you have made four squares. Every match has to form the side of a square.
● Remove two matches to create five squares.
● Move two matches so that you have made seven squares.
● Imagine this is a glass with a cherry in. You cannot touch the cherry (counter) but you have to move just two matches so that the cherry is outside the glass and the glass stays exactly the same shape.

ANSWERS

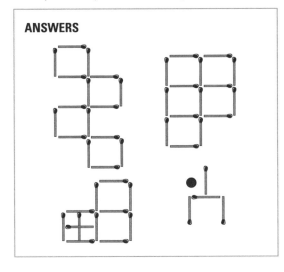

SILLY SENTENCES

THINKING SKILL: creative
SUBJECT LINK: literacy
LEARNING LINK: visual
ORGANISATION: groups of four
RESOURCES: small squares of paper for each team; pens; whiteboards

WHAT TO DO

● Each child needs a pen and a supply of small squares of paper. Each child in the group is allocated a number – one, two, three or four.
● Call out, *one noun, two verb, three adjective and four adverb.* All the children who are number one write a noun on their piece of paper, the number two's all write a verb and so on. The group then has 30 seconds to create a sentence using the four words they have come up with. Share these sentences with the whole class.
● For the next round, call out a different sentence part for each number.

MOOD MODELS

THINKING SKILL: creative
SUBJECT LINK: PSHE
LEARNING LINK: visual
ORGANISATION: individual
RESOURCES: modelling clay

WHAT TO DO

● Create a mind map of moods and emotions: tired, gloomy, excited, scared, uninspired, shy, embarrassed. Use a thesaurus to expand the list. Discuss with the class what situations might evoke any of these moods or feelings. Discuss the colours that you may associate with different moods – blue is commonly associated with sadness, green with jealousy, red with anger, for example. Develop these concepts. Relate different moods to objects – clouds, thorns on a rose bush and so on.
● The children use modelling clay to model an abstract representation of the mood they have chosen, either from the list or from one of their own ideas.

JIGSAW ART

THINKING SKILL: creative
SUBJECT LINK: art, literacy
LEARNING LINK: visual
ORGANISATION: individual or pairs
RESOURCES: art gallery postcards featuring people, cut up into a number of pieces to create a jigsaw (the choice of postcards could feature work by a wide range of artists from past to present or focus on one particular artist or theme); A4 cards with the name of the artist and title of the painting written on one side; glue; pens

WHAT TO DO

● The children stick the reconstructed postcard onto the blank side of the A4 card. This activity will focus them on the detail of the paintings.
● After reconstructing the postcards, discuss with the children what the people in the paintings may be thinking or saying.
● The children write these suggestions on the card in speech or thought bubbles around the edge of the postcard.
● Share the children's work.

NOW TRY THIS

The children should then research the background to their painting using the painter's name and the title of the picture. They can then assess how their own ideas matched up with what the artist had intended to portray.

OBJECT LESSONS

THINKING SKILL: enquiry
SUBJECT LINK: history
LEARNING LINK: auditory
ORGANISATION: individual
RESOURCES: a wide variety of objects from a sieve to a bar of soap; a pencil

WHAT TO DO

● Explain to the children who Johann Heinrich Pestalozzi was and the concept behind his ideas.

> *Johann Heinrich Pestalozzi was a Swiss educational reformer who believed that teaching should use the senses and that teachers should not simply try to implant knowledge, but should allow children to use their senses to help them learn. He introduced the concept of 'object lessons'.*

● Give each child an object. They should touch it, explore it, smell it and so on. Individuals then describe their object, talk about what it might be used for.
● The class can then join in, further developing ideas about each object: What would life be like without the object? What could be used instead? What might have been used before this object was invented?

NOW TRY THIS

Go to the object lessons website at www.objectlessons.org.uk and try out some interactive object lessons in any of the history, science and geography zones (a free trial is available and subscriptions can be made for a site licence using eLearning Credits).

THE CLEPSYDRA

THINKING SKILL: evaluative
SUBJECT LINK: history, mathematics, design and technology
LEARNING LINK: visual
ORGANISATION: pairs
RESOURCES: plenty of empty plastic bottles; yoghurt pots; means of making a small hole (safety note: the children will need to be carefully supervised when making holes in the containers); stopwatches

WHAT TO DO

● In Ancient Greek courts, the clepsydra (water clock) was used for timing speeches. Water was poured into a pot, which sat on a clay block. The pot had a small hole, which allowed the water to run out into another pot, placed carefully beneath the top pot. When the lower pot was full, the speaker's time had run out.
● The children use recycled materials to create their own clepsydra. The aim is to create a clepsydra that will run for approximately one minute.

NOW TRY THIS

Once the water clocks have been made, and the history unit on Ancient Greeks is drawing to a close, try them out! Children can defend themselves in a Greek court by speaking about Ancient Greece using the clepsydra to time them.

THE BORROWERS

THINKING SKILL: creative
SUBJECT LINK: literacy
LEARNING LINK: visual
ORGANISATION: small groups
RESOURCES: a shoebox for each group; *The Borrowers* by Mary Norton

WHAT TO DO

● Introduce the story to the class and read an excerpt from the book. The Borrowers are the Clock family, tiny, but human-like creatures that live under the floorboards of a manor house. They survive by 'borrowing' items and leftovers from humans.

● Each group should use their shoebox to create a room for the Clock family – Pod (the father), Homily (the mother) and Arrietty (their 14-year-old daughter). Find items around the classroom and at home that can be used as items of furniture for tiny people (not dolls' house furniture!) The room can then be used as a stimulus for writing an adventure story about how the family came by one or more of the different items.

ELECTRIC BOARD GAMES

THINKING SKILL: creative, enquiry
SUBJECT LINK: science
LEARNING LINK: visual
ORGANISATION: small groups
RESOURCES: A3 board; paper fasteners; plastic-coated wire; wire strippers; battery; crocodile clips; tape; buzzers or light bulbs

WHAT TO DO

● The children decide on some facts that they want to learn – in geography they may want to learn which capital city belongs to which country, in history they may want to learn the dates different monarchs ruled between, and so on.

● They then find ten pairs of answers, for example ten countries and their ten capital cities. They design their board to look attractive with the countries spread evenly down the left-hand side and the capital cities down the right-hand side (muddled up!) Next to each they push a paper fastener through the board.

● On the back of the board, they join the correct country to its capital city, by using plastic-coated wire, stripped on the ends, and wound around the relevant paper fasteners. Tape can be used over the fasteners to ensure they don't touch neighbouring wires.

● Display the boards on a shelf. Provide a battery, with a buzzer or light bulb and crocodile clips to make a circuit.

● For the capital city example, to test their knowledge, they touch one crocodile clip on a country and one on a capital city. If they are correct, the buzzer should sound or the bulb light up. If this doesn't happen, they need to try again.

BUILD A BRIDGE

THINKING SKILL: enquiry
SUBJECT LINK: design and technology
LEARNING LINK: visual
ORGANISATION: small groups of three or four
RESOURCES: lots of old newspapers and tape; textbooks of equal weight (for example, dictionaries) for testing

WHAT TO DO

● Create a mind map of all the sorts of bridges the children can think of. For example: suspension bridges, arch bridges, lifting bridges, beam bridges, swing bridges and so on.

● Set a time limit of 30 minutes. Invite the children to make a bridge between two chairs using only newspaper and tape. The winning bridge will be the design that supports the greatest load.

● After testing, discuss the structures used and why different designs worked or didn't work.

NOW TRY THIS

1. Ask the children to find lots of photographs of bridges around the world.
2. Make a display of the children's bridge designs and compare their structures with famous bridges from around the world.

FLOATING AND SINKING

THINKING SKILL: enquiry
SUBJECT LINK: science
LEARNING LINK: visual
ORGANISATION: small groups or pairs
RESOURCES: a ball of clay; a tank or bowl of water; a chart for recording results; a digital camera

WHAT TO DO

- Ask the children to do the following:
  - Put the ball of clay into the tank to see if it floats or sink.
  - Mould it into different shapes and test them out.
- Take a photograph of each test shape showing the result.
- Print out your photographs and use them to make an information poster to explain why objects float or sink.

ANSWER

Any object has to displace a weight of water equal to its own weight if it is going to float. If it can't, then the weight will be greater than the up-thrust of the water and the object will sink. A ball of clay will sink because it cannot displace a weight of water equal to its own weight. If it is moulded into a cup shape with a large surface area, it will float even though it weighs the same as previously. This is because it can displace more water in this form and can gain enough up-thrust to keep itself afloat.

SPROUTS

THINKING SKILL: information processing
SUBJECT LINK: mathematics
LEARNING LINK: visual
ORGANISATION: pairs
RESOURCES: pen and paper or whiteboard and marker pens

WHAT TO DO

- Mathematicians John H Conway and Michael S Paterson, who were both at Cambridge University, invented this game in 1967.
- Play starts by randomly drawing a few spots (say four) on a piece of paper. Players take it in turn to draw a line between two spots or in a loop from a spot to itself and then add another spot to the line
- A spot can have a maximum of three lines.
- The line may not cross another line. The player then adds another spot to the line.
- Once a spot has three lines from it, it is classed as 'dead'. A loop counts as two lines. The last player to make a move wins.

COLOUR COMPLEMENTS

THINKING SKILL: creative
SUBJECT LINK: art
LEARNING LINK: visual
ORGANISATION: individual
RESOURCES: red, blue and yellow paint; mixing palettes with 12 segments; brushes; card circle divided into 12 sections

WHAT TO DO:

- Children need the following knowledge to carry out this activity:

  The primary colours are red, blue and yellow. These colours cannot be made by mixing any other colours.

  Secondary colours are made by mixing primary colours together. The secondary colours are green, orange and purple.

  Tertiary colours are a combination of primary and secondary colours. They are named by putting the colour names together: red-orange, yellow-orange, blue-green, yellow–green, blue-purple, red-purple (or violet).

- The children then use this knowledge to create a colour wheel with 12 segments starting with the three primary colours and mixing the paints to create the secondary and tertiary colours.
- Think of names for the tertiary colours.

NOW TRY THIS

Complementary colours are the colours that are opposite each other on the colour wheel. When placed together they make both colours appear brighter. The Impressionists such as Monet, Renoir, Pissarro and Manet made use of complementary colours to give their finished pictures depth and radiance. Ask the children to find examples of their work on the internet and look for use of pairs of complementary colours. A good starting point is *Blue Dancers* by Edgar Degas.

MUSICAL CHAIRS

THINKING SKILL: information processing
SUBJECT LINK: music
LEARNING LINK: visual
ORGANISATION: individual
RESOURCES: a large blank plan of the layout of an orchestra (see below); individual sticky labels for the instruments of the orchestra (as listed below); colouring pencils

2 harps	26 violins
12 cellos	10 violas
1 cor anglais	2 oboes
2 flutes	1 piccolo
1 bass clarinet	3 clarinets
3 bassoons	8 double basses
2 timpani	1 glockenspiel
1 bass drum	1 side drum
1 pair cymbals	4 French horns
3 trumpets	3 trombones
1 tuba	

WHAT TO DO

● Hand out the 88 instrument labels to the class randomly and display the blank orchestra plan on a board. Explain that you are the conductor of the orchestra and you want to organise your musicians into the correct seating plan for tonight's performance.

● The first task is to colour code the instruments. Ask the children to colour stringed instruments red, woodwind yellow, brass blue and percussion green.

● Call out instructions (such as cellos at the front, on the left) and the children with the relevant instruments should come up and arrange their stickers in the correct place. Remember to clarify which side is left, and which is right.

NOW TRY THIS

1. This exercise could also be carried out as a kinaesthetic learning activity involving 22 children at a time.
2. Make 21 instrument labels and one conductor label and arrange seats in the shape of an orchestra.
3. A volunteer takes on the role of conductor and asks the orchestra to 'take their seats' by directing them to where he or she wishes to place them.
4. Those not involved could have the correct seating plan available so they can check whether the conductor knows his orchestra!

NEWSPAPER VIEWS

THINKING SKILL: evaluation
SUBJECT LINK: geography, literacy
LEARNING LINK: visual, auditory
ORGANISATION: small groups
RESOURCES: one copy of the same newspaper for each group; scissors; glue; one large sheet of paper per group

WHAT TO DO

● Make list of articles you wish the groups to locate in their newspaper. They should be thought provoking and warrant discussion at the children's level of understanding.

● As each article is located, they should cut it out, stick it on the large sheet of paper and read it together as a group.

● They should discuss and write their views around the articles, ready to share and compare with the other groups.

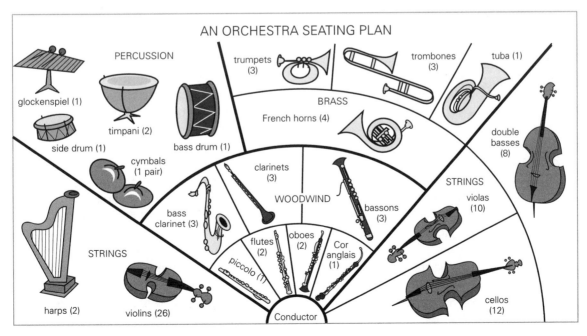

AN ORCHESTRA SEATING PLAN

A THERMOMETER

THINKING SKILL: enquiry
SUBJECT LINK: science
LEARNING LINK: visual
ORGANISATION: whole class
RESOURCES: a plastic bottle (not glass as it may shatter); balloon; bowl of very hot but not boiling water; bowl of ice cubes (safety note: take extra care with the hot water)

WHAT TO DO

● The children place a pre-stretched balloon over the mouth of an empty plastic bottle.
● They stand the bottle in the bowl of very hot water and observe what happens. Then they put the bottle into the bowl of ice cubes and again watch what happens.
● Ask them to draw a diagram of what they have seen.
● Can they explain what has happened?

ANSWER
The hot water heats up the air in the bottle, making it expand and therefore move out of the bottle into the balloon, thus starting to inflate it. The ice cools the air in the bottle down and makes it contract, so the balloon deflates again. This is how a thermometer works, but alcohol or mercury is used instead of water and a balloon!

HOW FAR?

THINKING SKILL: enquiry
SUBJECT LINK: geography
LEARNING LINK: visual
ORGANISATION: pairs
RESOURCES: OS maps – 1:25000 scale; string; rulers; pen and paper

WHAT TO DO

● Explain to the children that the scale of a map is the number of times you would have to enlarge your map to actually represent the real area it was showing. 1:25000 scale maps are the scale used by walkers. Explain to the children that 1cm on the map is equal to 25000cm or 250m or a quarter of a km. So 4cm on a 1:25000 scale OS map is equal to 1km.
● Ask them to find the distance between two places on the OS map using a piece of string. They need to hold the string at the starting point and bend it along the route until they arrive at the destination. They then mark or cut the string and measure it using a ruler.
● Calculate the distance of the route using either the scale bar or a ruler – a piece of string 8cm long would mean the distance was 2km.

NOW TRY THIS

1. Assume that a rambler walks on average 4 km/hour.
2. Ask the children to work out how long different routes would take based on this assumption.
3. They can then plan scenic routes for rambler groups, based on the idea that the trip should take eight hours including lunch breaks and rests or stops for sightseeing!

GREEK MYTH MODEL

THINKING SKILL: creative
SUBJECT LINK: history
LEARNING LINK: visual
ORGANISATION: small groups
RESOURCES: card; colouring materials; scissors; tissue paper; paints; recyclable materials and so on.

WHAT TO DO

● Read the myth of Jason, the Argonauts and the Golden Fleece with the class. A simplified version suitable for this task can be found at www.mythweb.com/heroes/jason.
● Allocate a different part of the myth to each group and explain that they will be creating a 3D model to retell the story. Each group should determine where their part of the story took place.
● To get an overview of the myth, create a simple storyboard with the children so that they can see what happens at a glance.
● Create a 3D base first: decide the general layout as a class, having discussed all the different parts of the myth in sequence.
● Once this has been made, each group makes stand-up characters cut out from card for their part of the story and cue cards to put on the storyboard. One group will each be responsible for making the cut-out of Jason; his ship the Argo; and his crew the Argonauts.
● The model, its cue cards and characters can then be used as a living story book – each group using the storyboard and the characters they have made to retell the myth in sequence.

A GREEK TIMELINE

THINKING SKILL: information processing
SUBJECT LINK: history
LEARNING LINK: visual
ORGANISATION: pairs
RESOURCES: timeline details; cards; string and pegs; the internet.,CD-ROMs; the library

WHAT TO DO

● Find a timeline of events in the history of Ancient Greece. An excellent example can be found at: www.bbc.co.uk/schools/ancientgreece/timeline (this timeline lists 15 key dates – ideal for a class of 30 working in pairs.)
● Allocate a date for each pair to research. Use the internet, CD-ROMS and the library to locate relevant pictures for each event. Each pair will create a card with pictures and captions for the date they have been given. When complete, the class have to physically organise their cards by hanging them on a washing line across the classroom.

COIN CONUNDRUM

THINKING SKILL: reasoning
SUBJECT LINK: mathematics
LEARNING LINK: visual
ORGANISATION: individual
RESOURCES: four counters; a square drawn on a piece of paper

WHAT TO DO

● The children place each of their four counters on each of the four vertices of the square.
● They make another square by moving only two of the counters – they do not touch the other two!

ANSWER

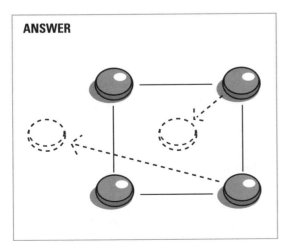

SOCKS

THINKING SKILL: creative
SUBJECT LINK: art, literacy
LEARNING LINK: visual
ORGANISATION: six groups
RESOURCES: 'Socks' by John Coldwell; sock outline on art paper (A3) copied for each child; paints; foils; tissue paper

Socks

On Monday we wear quiet socks,
Not flash, bang, start a riot socks,
Not, Hey you come and try it socks.
On Monday we wear quiet socks.

On Tuesday we wear plain socks,
Not crazy and insane socks,
Not frazzle up your brain socks.
On Tuesday we wear plain socks.

On Wednesday we wear boring socks,
Not pass to me goal scoring socks,
Not Pollock's abstract drawing socks.
On Wednesday we wear boring socks

On Thursday. Ordinary socks,
Not horror, shock and scarey socks,
Not beastly monsters hairy socks.
On Thursday. Ordinary socks.

On Friday, it's polite socks.
Not glowing in the night socks,
Not give your aunt a fright socks,
On Friday it's polite socks.

At weekends we wear loud socks,
That stand out in the crowd socks
And make our feet feel proud socks.
At weekends we wear loud socks.

John Coldwell

WHAT TO DO

● Read the poem 'Socks' by John Coldwell. There are 18 different types of socks described.
● Allocate a verse to each of the six groups.
● They should design a pair of socks for each of the three descriptions contained in their verse. For example, verse one will require a pair of 'quiet socks', a pair of 'flash, bang start a riot socks' and a pair of 'Hey you, come and try it socks'.
● Display the final designs and the poem, suspended from the ceiling.

NEWSPAPER HUNT

THINKING SKILL: enquiry
SUBJECT LINK: geography, literacy
LEARNING LINK: visual
ORGANISATION: small groups
RESOURCES: one copy of the same newspaper for each group; scissors; glue; one large sheet of paper per group; highlighters

WHAT TO DO

● On the board write up ten pieces of information you wish the children to find in their newspapers.
● The children are to cut out the relevant articles, stick it onto their large sheet of paper and highlight the pieces of information.
● The first group to complete their 'Newspaper Hunt' is the winner.
● Ensure that in preparing the search, pieces of information are not on the back of each other!

ALPHABET AUTHORS

THINKING SKILL: evaluation
SUBJECT LINK: literacy
LEARNING LINK: visual
ORGANISATION: individual
RESOURCES: green paper; compasses; scissors; black pens; treasury tags; lists of suggested children's authors

WHAT TO DO

● This is an ongoing challenge that is best started at the beginning of the year.
● Each child will need to cut out 27 circles of green paper and a triangle. One circle will be used to create a caterpillar head and the rest will be the segments of its body – one segment for each letter of the alphabet.
● They should begin by drawing a cartoon face and then join the circles together using treasury tags, writing one letter of the alphabet on each. Add the triangle at the end for the tail.
● Fold the caterpillar up in a concertina style. Display the caterpillars around the class where they can be reached. One option is to create a large leaf-shaped book and keep the caterpillars in pockets on the pages – one page for each child. Alternatively, increase the tactile element by making felt leaf-shaped pockets for the caterpillars.
● Every time a book or poem is read, the segment of the caterpillar corresponding to the author's surname is completed. For example, after reading *Tom's Midnight Garden* by Philippa
● Pearce you would complete the section 'P' on the caterpillar. If you then read a poem by John Foster, the 'F' section could be completed. There could be a small reward for the person who completes his or her caterpillar first.

NOW TRY THIS

Create a large caterpillar for the class to fill in together. Display it on the wall so children can share the books that they have read.

GLOSSARY GAMES

THINKING SKILL: reasoning
SUBJECT LINK: geography
LEARNING LINK: visual
ORGANISATION: teams
RESOURCES: word and definition cards relating to rivers, coasts and mountains; a hoop for each team; a score board

WHAT TO DO

● Place all the cards face up in the centre of the hall. Each team is lined up behind a hoop.
● Blow the whistle to start, the first team member runs up and collects a pair of cards – one word and one definition, and places them in the team hoop.
● The whistle is blown again to signal the end of the round.
● Each team calls out their pair – if a correct word and definition has been made the team scores a point.
● If the pairing is incorrect the cards are replaced.
● The second player then takes a turn and so on. The team with the highest number of correct words and definition pairs is the winner.
● This may be played at the end of the year using terms from several schemes of work or at the end of each study unit.

JIGSAW JUGGLING

THINKING SKILL: enquiry, creative thinking
SUBJECT LINK: mathematics
LEARNING LINK: visual
ORGANISATION: individual
RESOURCES: squares of paper and scissors; a variety of different types of jigsaw puzzle pieces

WHAT TO DO

● Jigsaw pieces may have zero, one or two straight edges, and different combinations of knobs and holes.
● Distribute the puzzle pieces around the class and look at and feel all the different shapes of the pieces. Ask the children to make 18 different shapes of jigsaw pieces by cutting shapes out of paper.

ANSWER

www.brainboxx.co.uk

CLOUD SPOTTING

THINKING SKILL: information processing
SUBJECT LINK: geography
LEARNING LINK: visual
ORGANISATION: groups
RESOURCES: index cards; photographs of eight main types of clouds; facts about cloud types

WHAT TO DO

● Explain how clouds are formed and that there are three main kinds – cumulus, stratus and cirrus. Each group will need eight index cards. They should label each card with the name of the cloud type: cumulus, altocumulus, cirrocumulus and cumulonimbus, stratus,

altostratus and cirrostratus and cirrus. They then print a photograph of each type and stick this onto the card, or draw a picture of the cloud type. They write a brief explanation of how each type is formed on the card.
● Go out with the class on cloudy days and use the cards to see what types of clouds are in the sky. Use the cards throughout the day to see how the clouds change. Use the explanations of how each cloud is formed to explain what is happening with the weather.

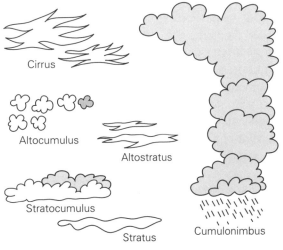

Cirrus

Altocumulus

Altostratus

Stratocumulus

Stratus

Cumulonimbus

PONG HAU K'I

THINKING SKILL: reasoning, evaluation
SUBJECT LINK: mathematics
LEARNING LINK: visual
ORGANISATION: pairs
RESOURCES: playing board and two (different coloured) painted stones for each player (you can make your playing board on paper or draw it on the playground in chalk)

WHAT TO DO

● This game originated in China. The aim of the game is to block your opponent and prevent them from moving.
● One player places his/her two stones on the two points on the left-hand side of the

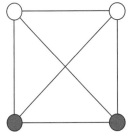

board and the other player places his/her stones on the two points on the right-hand side of the board.
● Players take it in turn to move their pieces along the lines into the next empty point.
● The winner is the player who blocks their opponent and prevents them from making a move.

WORD PROBLEM

THINKING SKILL: enquiry
SUBJECT LINK: mathematics
LEARNING LINK: visual
ORGANISATION: individual
RESOURCES: word processing package; card; laminator

WHAT TO DO

● Prepare a card for each child to help them adopt a methodical approach when solving word problems in mathematics.

Involve the children in making the card to encourage a sense of 'ownership' of the methodology.

● Laminate the cards to ensure that they are long-lasting.

● Write the children's names on the cards.

A suggestion for the card might be:

Solving word problems
Six steps to remember:
Read the question twice.
Underline the key information (unless in a text book in which case jot down!)
Identify the calculation(s) needed.
Estimate the answer.
Decide on the method for calculating.
Check the answer – does it make sense?

MANKALA

THINKING SKILL: evaluation, reasoning
SUBJECT LINK: mathematics
LEARNING LINK: visual
ORGANISATION: pairs
RESOURCES: for each game set: egg carton (for a dozen eggs!) with the lid removed; two extra cups – one taped to each end of the carton; paints; 36 beans or similar

WHAT TO DO

● Allow pairs to make their own Mankala board and playing pieces by painting and decorating their egg cartons.

● Place three beans in each cup on the board.

● Players sit facing one side of the board, the cups on that side are their cups and they have the end cup to their right as their scoring cup.

● The first player chooses one cup and takes the beans from it. Each bean is placed, one at a time, into the successive cups, moving anti-clockwise around the board. Beans placed in the end cup on the player's right are points for that player. Do not place beans in the opponent's scoring cup.

● If the last bean in a play is placed in the player's own cup, they get another turn. If the last bean is placed in an empty cup on their own side of the board, then they capture the beans in the opposite (their opponent's) cup.

● All captured beans, as well as the capturing piece, are placed in the player's scoring cup. When all of the cups on one side of the board are empty the game is over.

● The player who has any beans left over gets to put them in their own scoring cup. The winner is the player with the most beans.

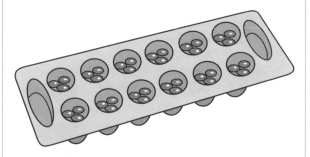

ACHI

THINKING SKILL: reasoning, evaluation
SUBJECT LINK: mathematics
LEARNING LINK: visual
ORGANISATION: pairs
RESOURCES: an Achi board drawn on paper or on the pavement in chalk; four counters for each player

WHAT TO DO

● This game comes from Ghana and is similar to noughts and crosses.

● In the first phase of the game, players take it in turn to place their counters on the board until all eight counters have been placed.

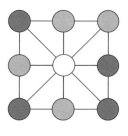

● In the second phase, players take it in turn to move a counter along a line to a new point.

● The winner is the first player to make a line of three counters of their own colour – horizontally, vertically or diagonally.

DOMINOES FIVES AND THREES

THINKING SKILL: evaluation
SUBJECT LINK: mathematics
LEARNING LINK: visual
ORGANISATION: small groups
RESOURCES: sets of dominoes; pen and paper

WHAT TO DO

● Divide the dominoes equally – any spares form a pool. You might like to have a non-playing scorekeeper in each team.
● The player throwing the highest double starts. A chain is formed by players adding a piece to either end of the chain – matching one of their pieces to one of the pieces on the chain. If they cannot match a piece they pick a piece from the pool or miss a turn.
● Points are scored when the total spots at the end of the chain add up to a multiple of five or three. For example, if the spots add up to nine the player scores three points, if they add up to ten they score two points. If the spots add up to 15 the player scores eight points (5 + 3).
● The first player to use up all his/her pieces collects ten extra points and one point for each piece not yet played.

LIVING MAPS

THINKING SKILL: reasoning
SUBJECT LINK: geography
LEARNING LINK: visual
ORGANISATION: small groups
RESOURCES: aerial photographs of the local area (enlarged to A3 size); small pieces of card; pens; small stickers

WHAT TO DO

● Each group is given an aerial photograph showing their school and the surrounding area.
● The group should make ten statement cards relating to specific points on the photograph.
● Five of these should be factual and five should be opinion. For example, one card may say 'This is the swimming pool' (fact), whereas the second card may say 'This area is an eye sore and needs improving' (opinion). They should then number the cards and use small stickers to number the relevant location on the photograph.

● As a whole class, compare the statements of different groups to see what opinions were formed about the local area.

SORT IT

THINKING SKILL: evaluation
SUBJECT LINK: design and technology
LEARNING LINK: visual
ORGANISATION: pairs or small groups
RESOURCES: dried lentils, peas and beans; recycled containers such as polystyrene trays and cardboard boxes; means of making holes in the containers, such as craft knives or pencils (safety note: the children will need to be carefully supervised when making holes in the containers)

WHAT TO DO

● Provide each group with a cup full of mixed peas, beans and lentils and ask them to design and make a device for separating them into three piles.

WORD TREE

THINKING SKILL: information processing
SUBJECT LINK: literacy
LEARNING LINK: visual
ORGANISATION: individual
RESOURCES: tree trunk and branches drawn on large piece of paper and mounted on accessible wall; envelope full of cut-out green leaves pinned next to tree; Blu-Tack

WHAT TO DO

● Make the word tree part of everyday life in class to provide a new focus each week.
● If the word-level objective is to learn words containing a certain letter string such as –ough, make a title card for the tree with this letter string on.
● Explain to the children that every time a word containing –ough is found or thought of (during reading, at home, during conversation and so on) they can go to the tree, take a leaf, write the word and their name on the leaf and stick the leaf onto a branch.
● Before a new word-level objective is introduced, read all the leaves out and celebrate good examples. Peel the leaves from the tree and stick them in a project book. Give the word tree a new title and begin again the next week. Children can take responsibility for keeping a good stock of new leaves.

KINAESTHETIC LEARNING

PIRATE ISLAND

THINKING SKILL: evaluation
SUBJECT LINK: PE
LEARNING LINK: visual
ORGANISATION: groups
RESOURCES: PE equipment (benches, mats, climbing frame and so on); a large number of balls of different sizes; beanbags; large box or bag; whiteboard and marker for scoring; stopwatch

WHAT TO DO

● The hall or gymnasium floor represents shark-infested waters, which is forbidden territory. The P.E equipment and mats are the desert islands, which are rugged and treacherous. They should be placed a reasonable distance apart, yet should be close enough for the children to step onto the pieces of equipment safely. Balls and beanbags form the 'treasure' and one mat with a box on it represents the pirate ship and the ships treasure hold.

● Spread the 'treasure' around the 'islands' in the shark-infested water.

● Each team is given a set time (depending on the scale of equipment used) to collect as much treasure as they can and return to the ship. Any pirate not back on board when the time is up incurs a major penalty for their team. The treasure is to be collected in the treasure hold on the ship.

● Predetermine a point system for each type of treasure, for example, three points for a large ball, two points for a small ball, and so on. Decide how many points to deduct should a pirate step into the water or not be on board ship at the end of the team's treasure hunt.

● This activity encourages the children to work together and demonstrates that individual speed can be slower than steady teamwork.

WITNESS FIRST HAND

THINKING SKILL: creative
SUBJECT LINK: geography, literacy
ORGANISATION: whole class or individuals
RESOURCES: *Earthquake* by Ruskin Bond (Walker Books): three children and their grandparents witness and survive an earthquake in a busy little hill town in North-Eastern India; *Hero* by Allan Baillie (Puffin): three children who dislike each other have to face up to the challenges and dangers of the rising waters of the Sydney floods of 1986 together; *The Boy from Sula* by Lavinia Derwent (Floris Books): Magnus Macduff's island of Sula is under threat of development

WHAT TO DO

● Approach issues of global importance and bring dramatic events such as floods or earthquakes into the realms of children's understanding by using fiction to demonstrate the effects on people's lives.

● As a class, read a story together which is relevant to your current scheme of work in geography (suggested examples are given above).

● Select a particular key event in the story. In the hall, children work as individuals.

● Recap a chosen event – call out *Action!* The children must adopt a character and mime the action described, concentrating on the feelings of the character.

● When you call out *Freeze*, they hold their position at that moment.

● Walk around and tap individuals on the shoulder. If tapped, they should say who they are, what they are doing and how they are feeling.

● Continue with the next sequence of events, calling *Action* at appropriate points and freezing the action again as appropriate.

DIGITAL PHOTO TRAIL

THINKING SKILL: creative, evaluation
SUBJECT LINK: art, outdoor and adventurous activities
LEARNING LINK: visual
ORGANISATION: an even number of small groups
RESOURCES: digital camera; printer and paper; cards for secret messages

WHAT TO DO

● Each group is given an allocated time to use the digital camera to take ten photographs of objects around the school from obscure angles. The angle of the photograph should make it difficult but not impossible to identify the object.

● They then print the photographs and mount them on card. The photographs are numbered one to ten.

● The group keeps photograph one. This is used as the starting clue for the photo trail. Photograph two is hidden at the location of the item in photograph one; photograph three is hidden at the location of the item in photograph two and so on.

● A card with a secret message written on is hidden at the location of the item in photograph ten. The children could use a simple code such as numbers for letters to write this message.

● Once all the groups have created their photo cards and secret messages, the trails can be laid. Groups swap photograph one and follow the trails to see who can find the secret message in the shortest time.

KEEPING TRACK

THINKING SKILL: information processing
SUBJECT LINK: PE, outdoor and adventurous activities
ORGANISATION: small groups
RESOURCES: sticks; pebbles

WHAT TO DO

● Tracking is a traditional scouting activity in which groups leave a trail of tracking signs for others to follow.

● Teach the children the common tracking signs which use sticks and stones. (Do not break sticks from living plants – always use dead wood.)

● Groups then leave trails for other groups to follow.

● This can be carried out around the school or in another location. Ensure that groups are supervised by responsible adults.

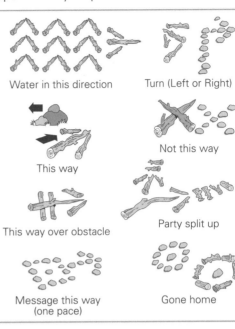

Water in this direction — Turn (Left or Right) — This way — Not this way — This way over obstacle — Party split up — Message this way (one pace) — Gone home

DICE RELAY

THINKING SKILL: information processing, evaluation
SUBJECT LINK: mathematics
LEARNING LINK: visual, auditory
ORGANISATION: two teams
RESOURCES: two dice for each team; two hoops; pen and paper; playing field

WHAT TO DO

● Each team nominates a leader. The team works out which numbers can be rolled with two dice and writes down a list of ten of these numbers (numbers can be repeated).

● Check the list of each team. The teams line up one behind the other. The dice are placed about 20 metres away inside a hoop – one for each team.

● The activity starts. The first team member runs up, shakes the dice, calls out the two numbers and their sum – if it is on the list the team leader crosses it off. Watch to ensure fair play!

● The winning team is the first to cross off all ten numbers. Was the result luck or down to mathematical probability? Try the game again and then discuss the choices of numbers in a maths lesson on probability.

NOW TRY THIS

Use the product of the numbers rather than the total. Try the game with three dice. How long does it take?

HERCULEAN SCULPTURES

THINKING SKILL: creative
SUBJECT LINK: history, literacy
LEARNING LINK: visual
ORGANISATION: twelve groups
RESOURCES: The myth 'The Labours of Hercules' (a suitable simplified version of this can be found at www.mythweb.com)

WHAT TO DO

● The class creates a series of tableaux to symbolise the Labours of Hercules.
● Allocate each group one of the labours of Hercules to read and discuss.
● Write an inscription using concise and appropriate language, which is to be placed next to the sculpture.
● The group then forms into a human sculpture symbolising the event. For example, Hercules' first labour was to kill the Nemean lion. Several children could form the cave in which Hercules throttled the lion, one child could take on the role of the slain lion on the floor of the cave and another child could be Hercules towering over the lion, his hands about to throttle the lion – both adopting appropriate expressions. Ensure this is carried out safely!

HOW DOES IT FEEL?

THINKING SKILL: evaluation
LEARNING LINK: auditory
SUBJECT LINK: citizenship
ORGANISATION: groups and pairs
RESOURCES: PE equipment; blindfolds

WHAT TO DO

● In groups, the children first discuss how different their lives would be if they could not see. Encourage them to think about how they would cope with different everyday tasks, how their free time would change, how they would cope with school and how they would have to rely on other people. Discuss the concepts of trust and empathy.

● Put the children into pairs and set up a course of obstacles. One member of each pair is blindfolded. Their partner's job is to verbally guide them around the obstacle course.
● Partners then swap roles.
● Follow this activity with a discussion of how it felt to be the 'blind' person and how it felt to have the responsibility of guiding their partner.

PORT/STARBOARD

THINKING SKILL: information processing, creative
SUBJECT LINK: literacy (speaking and listening); geography (directions)
LEARNING LINK: auditory
ORGANISATION: whole class
RESOURCES: large space

WHAT TO DO

● Nominate a captain of the ship. The captain calls out instructions. The last child to complete the action is out and helps the captain to spot other slack crewmembers! The instructions are as follows:

> *Port* – *run to left hand wall*
> *Starboard* – *run to right hand wall*
> *Captain's coming* – *stand and salute*
> *Admiral* – *stand still and play the flute*
> *Man the lifeboats* – *safely get off the ground*
> *Climb the rigging* – *pretend to climb a rope*
> *Scrub the decks* – *pretend to scrub the floor*
> *Sharks* – *lie on the floor with legs in the air*
> *Bombs overhead* – *lie on floor with hands over head*
> *Captain's wife* – *stand and bow or curtsey.*

NOW TRY THIS

Children work in groups of five or six to create their own version of the game. Provide starting points such as 'The Country Code' or 'Outward Bounds'.

CHARADES

THINKING SKILL: creative
SUBJECT LINK: literacy
LEARNING LINK: visual
ORGANISATION: whole class in two teams
RESOURCES: a list of books, songs, TV programmes and films known to the class written individually on strips of card; stopwatch

WHAT TO DO

● A volunteer from Team A comes to the front of the class, selects a strip of card and then proceeds to mime out its title.
● First he/she indicates how many words are in the title by holding up the appropriate number of fingers.
● The category is then indicated as follows:

> *Book:*
> unfold hands as if opening a book
> *Film:*
> wind up an old fashioned camera (explain the relevance of this to the class)
> *TV:*
> draw a square in the air to represent a TV screen

● Next, the child mimes out the title using the following signals to help:

> *Sounds like:*
> cup hand to ear
> *Small word:*
> use thumb and index finger to indicate 'tiny'
> *Number of the word about to be mimed:*
> hold up that number of fingers
> *To break a word into syllables:*
> put the number of fingers equal to the number of syllables in the word, on the forearm.
> *To indicate which syllable is to be mimed next:*
> tap that number of fingers on the forearm.
> *To indicate the past tense:*
> point over shoulder.

● Decide how long is allowed for each charade. If nobody from Team B guesses correctly, it is passed over to the volunteer's own team to guess (who should keep quiet during the mime). A correct guess should be awarded ten points.
● A volunteer from Team B then does their mime.
● Continue for a set number of rounds. The team with the highest score wins.

FIND THE ANGLE

THINKING SKILL: information processing
SUBJECT LINK: mathematics
LEARNING LINK: visual
ORGANISATION: individual
RESOURCES: protractors; pens and paper

WHAT TO DO

● Each child draws a table like the one below and uses it to record the location, type and measurement of angles they find in and around their classroom.
● Encourage the children to explore the classroom thoroughly to find as many different angles as they can.

Location	Measurement	Acute?	Right angle?	Obtuse?

ALPHABET SHUFFLE

THINKING SKILL: information processing
SUBJECT LINK: PE
ORGANISATION: groups
RESOURCES: PE benches

WHAT TO DO

● Space out four benches across the hall or gym space.
● Split the class into four groups. The groups stand themselves on the benches.
● When the whistle is blown, the groups have to organise themselves into alphabetical order by first name – without stepping off the bench!
● The children have to work out who is to go at the front, then second and so on, and work together to move along the bench without falling into the 'shark-infested' waters below. Any team who steps off the bench is out.

NOW TRY THIS

To vary this exercise, the children can organise themselves by age or by the number of letters in their whole name.

OOPS BOX

THINKING SKILL: evaluation
SUBJECT LINK: literacy
LEARNING LINK: visual, auditory
ORGANISATION: individual
RESOURCES: large colourful box with lid; supply of Oops! Cards (see below); gold or silver pen to stay in box

Oops! card:

> **Oops !**
>
> Spelling error: _____
>
> Correct spelling: _____
>
> Name: _____
>
> Date: _____

WHAT TO DO

● If a spelling error is found when marking, underline the spelling and write 'Oops!' in the margin. When the children are given their books back after marking, the first thing they should do at the beginning of the lesson is 'do their Oops! Cards'. For each 'Oops!', they should take a blank Oops! card and complete it – finding out the correct spelling by using a dictionary, spell checker or whatever methods are employed in class. They then place the completed Oops! card in the Oops! box.

● Periodically, at the end of a lesson invite someone to collect the Oops! box and select a card. They read out the name of the person and the word that was incorrectly spelt. The person responds by verbally spelling the word. If they are correct, the card goes in the bin, if not the card is returned to the box for another session, and the correct spelling is then established by the class and written on the board. Another card is then chosen and the exercise repeated.

WHAT I LEARNED TODAY!

THINKING SKILL: information processing, evaluation
SUBJECT LINK: all
LEARNING LINK: auditory
ORGANISATION: individual
RESOURCES: board; strips of paper and pens

WHAT TO DO

● At the end of every day, make time to carry out this activity, which will encourage the children to reflect on their learning and help to consolidate what has been learned.

● Write up the question 'What have we learned today?' in a big thought bubble on the board.

● Everybody writes something they have personally learned on a strip of paper and comes up, reads it out and sticks it around the speech bubble. Encourage the children to pay attention and to listen to each other.

● Vote on which learning objective was the most relevant/interesting/challenging. When everyone has contributed and shared their thoughts it is time to go home and relate what they have learned to their parents or carers.

MAGIC CARPET

THINKING SKILL: creative
SUBJECT LINK: geography, history
LEARNING LINK: auditory
ORGANISATION: whole class or groups
RESOURCES: PE mats; mood music

WHAT TO DO

● Create a magic carpet for the class to sit on either as a whole class or small groups (if confident in drama situations).

● Set the scene: you have discovered a dusty old carpet in an eccentric elderly aunt's attic. The carpet is magic and takes you on a journey, flying high up into the sky. It swoops down, hovering and circling over your featured location/situation. Choose either an event being studied in history or a location in geography.

● The children take on the situation and use gestures and words to point out what is happening. Encourage the use of relevant geographical or historical vocabulary.

● As the children become more immersed in the drama, encourage them to guide the carpet to swoop in to get up close, escape quickly from danger and hover over beautiful scenery.

● Encourage detailed descriptions by prompting and questioning – other children can prompt and question too.

● This can be used as an excellent assessment opportunity – as it will reveal information the children have learnt during the study unit.

SANDWICH SPELLING

THINKING SKILL: information processing
SUBJECT LINK: literacy
LEARNING LINK: visual
ORGANISATION: three teams
RESOURCES: three rows of ten chairs, set up on different sides of the hall or a large open space; three sets of ten A4 cards – each card with a single letter on it spelling the word 'SANDWICHES' (if you have fewer than 30 children either create your own version of the game or allow certain children to have responsibility for more than one letter. If there are more than 30 children, some may take on the roles of question master and scorekeepers); question sheet; a scoreboard and pen

WHAT TO DO

● Choose a team leader for each team. The team decides on a team name based on a sandwich filling, for example: cheese and pickle or peanut butter. Teams sit on the row of chairs allocated to them, holding their letters facing the front, so they spell out the word 'SANDWICHES'.

● The question master reads out a clue. When the team has worked out the answer, the team leader collects the children with the letters required to spell out the answer and he/she organises them into the correct order in front of the question master. For example: *You need to do this to your food before you swallow.* The answer is CHEW so the team leader organises the children with the letters C, H, E and W in front of the judge.

● The first team to be standing spelling the answer to the clue in front of the question

master scores a point. The winning team is the team with the highest number of points.

Question sheet:
1. *Fine grains resulting from the erosion of rocks. (SAND)*
2. *Continuous dull pain. (ACHE)*
3. *Sour. (ACID)*
4. *Twelve of these make a foot. One of these is the same as 2.54cm. (INCH)*
5. *A country in the continent of Asia. (CHINA)*
6. *Crank of wheel or axle. (WINCH)*
7. *The sound a curtain makes. (SWISH)*
8. *You do this to music. (DANCE)*
9. *A game played on a black and white board. (CHESS)*
10. *A cube with six numbers on. (DICE)*
11. *To reflect light. (SHINE)*
12. *Daybreak. (DAWN)*
13. *The part of your body on top of your neck. (HEAD)*
14. *Very clever or sensible. (WISE)*
15. *A plan. (IDEA)*
16. *To look over something very quickly. (SCAN)*
17. *A good place to sit to keep cool on a hot sunny day. (SHADE)*
18. *Dogs and children do this when they are unhappy! (WHINE)*
19. *To walk through water or mud with difficulty. (WADE)*
20. *A connected series of links. (CHAIN)*

Other words you could make up clues for include: acne, anew, case, cash, Chad, dash, disc, dine, hide, hind, hiss, iced, nice, said, sane, sash, sawn, send, shed, shin, side, swan, wand, wash, wind, anise, ashen, aside, chase, chide, niche, shied, since, swine, widen, wince.

A SENSE OF PLACE

THINKING SKILL: creative
SUBJECT LINK: art
LEARNING LINK: visual, tactile
ORGANISATION: individual, small groups or whole class
RESOURCES: natural materials

WHAT TO DO

● Introduce the work of Andrew Goldsworthy to the class and view his works online. www.sculpture.org.uk.

● Discuss how he uses natural materials in a natural setting to create his sculptures. The children create an ephemeral structure using natural materials that are available.

BRITISH SIGN LANGUAGE

THINKING SKILL: information processing, creative
SUBJECT LINK: PSHE
LEARNING LINK: visual
ORGANISATION: whole class and pairs
RESOURCES: British Sign Language (BSL) information literature, such as leaflets, posters, postcards; online British Sign Language websites such as www.learnbsl.org and www.deafsign.com (which have useful educational movies demonstrating the BSL alphabet (finger spelling), phrases, signs for words and so on); a visitor who can sign

WHAT TO DO

● Demonstrate and practice the BSL alphabet (also known as finger spelling) and common useful phrases. The children can then practise spelling out their names.

● Learn some useful instruction phrases as a whole class, which can be used on a daily basis when the class needs settling down or bringing together.

Good, Great, Hello
Closed hand (or both hands) with thumb up makes short movement forward.

Hello, Hi
Flat hand with thumb tucked in makes short movement out from near side of head.

Please, Thanks
Tips of flat hand touch mouth, then hand swings forward/down to finish palm up.

Quick, Fast, Hurry
Right index taps on left index several times very quickly.

Quiet/ly, Hush, Sh
Index finger to lips, 'O' hands then touch, and then swing slightly down and apart slowly.

How are you?
Tips of hands on chest; hands move forward closing with thumbs up, eyebrows raised.

© Co-Sign communications

DIGIT DILEMMAS

THINKING SKILL: information processing
SUBJECT LINK: mathematics
LEARNING LINK: visual, auditory
ORGANISATION: three teams of ten spread out in a large space (hall or school field)
RESOURCES: three sets of large number cards (numbered 0 to 9); a scoreboard and pen; chalk (to create an answer box on the floor for each team); whiteboard and pen for each team

WHAT TO DO

● The class is split into three teams and each team nominates a team leader. You also need a question master (either yourself or nominate a child). Each team member has a number card and sits in a row in numerical order.

● The question master calls out a question. The teams work out the answer and the team leaders organise their team into the correct order, holding the relevant number cards, and send them to the team answer box.

● The first team standing with the correct answer in their box is awarded a point. At the end of the game, the team with the highest score wins.

SAMPLE QUESTIONS (WITH ANSWERS)
1. How many minutes in 4½ hours? (270 minutes)
2. There are 270 children in a school. A third are girls, how many boys are there? (180)
3. Subtract 445 from 598. (153)
4. 6 pots each contain 49 buttons. How many buttons altogether? (294)
5. A bag of sand weighs 56kg. A bucket holds 2kg. How many buckets of sand will the bag fill? (28)
6. What is ninety thousand eight hundred and sixty two in numerals? (90862)
7. Crisps cost £1.56 for 6 packets, but there is an offer of 'Buy one pack, get one pack free'. What is the price of each bag of crisps with this special offer? (13p)
8. Find 30% of 330. (10% is 33 so 30% is 33 × 3 = 99)
9. You cycle 5km to the swimming pool, which is 33m long. You swim 6 lengths and then cycle home. How many metres have you cycled and swum altogether? (5000 + 5000 + 198 = 10,198m)
10. I am two digits. The product of my digits is (25 × 2) + 6. The sum of my digits is 15 and my digits are two consecutive numbers. I am > 50 but < 100. (78)

ADVERB ACTIONS

THINKING SKILL: creative
SUBJECT LINK: literacy
LEARNING LINK: visual
ORGANISATION: individuals in front of whole class
RESOURCES: whiteboard and pen; thesauruses; cards

WHAT TO DO

● Brainstorm a list of adverbs and use a thesaurus to expand the list further. Write the adverbs on the board.
● Cover the list of adverbs and make duplicate cards for each one.
● Choose a volunteer to start. The volunteer selects an adverb card.
● A class member suggests an action such as clean your teeth, in the manner of the adverb.
● The volunteer carries out the mime and the class have to guess the adverb.

WHO GOES THERE?

THINKING SKILL: information processing
SUBJECT LINK: speaking and listening
LEARNING LINK: auditory
ORGANISATION: whole class
RESOURCES: blindfold; drum and drumstick

WHAT TO DO

● The class stands in a circle with one person blindfolded, standing in the middle. He or she is the guard at Buckingham Palace.
● The guard beats the drum and the class march around in a circle until the beating stops.
● The guard points with the drumstick and asks, *Who approaches the Palace?* The person replies with the name of a famous person.
● The guard then guesses the true identity of the speaker. If correct, they have another turn as the guard, if not they swap places with the person who foiled the guard.

ANTIQUES ROADSHOW

THINKING SKILL: enquiry
SUBJECT LINK: history
LEARNING LINK: visual, tactile
ORGANISATION: groups
RESOURCES: excerpt from the *Antiques Roadshow* on video; the children bring in items (toys, kitchen equipment, records, and so on) for the 'roadshow' (with the permission of the owner – suggest non-breakable) which are typical of the period 1948 – about 1980

WHAT TO DO

● Watch the *Antiques Roadshow* excerpt so that everyone is aware of the format of the show.
● Ask the groups to prepare for the activity by bringing in items from the decades between the 1940s and the 1980s. They should find out about the objects, what they were used for, their popularity, cost, and what superseded each item.
● When everyone in each group is familiar with the object and its history, decide which group members are going to be the 'experts' and prepare a programme for the rest of the class to watch.

MINIBEAST MAGNET

THINKING SKILL: evaluation
SUBJECT LINK: science
LEARNING LINK: visual
ORGANISATION: whole class and individual
RESOURCES: dead wood and bark; pooters (or glass jars and other containers); magnifying glasses; identification keys

WHAT TO DO

● Help the children to create a log pile in a suitable spot in the school grounds. Dead wood provides a home and shelter for a whole range of minibeasts, such as woodlice, beetles, worms and so on.
● Ask them to create a sign informing the rest of the school what the area is for. Once established, visit the area as a class and carefully lift up pieces of the wood to observe and record what you can see.

CONSTELLATION CAPERS

THINKING SKILL: creative
SUBJECT LINK: history, science
LEARNING LINK: visual, tactile
ORGANISATION: whole class
RESOURCES: a large sheet of black paper with chalk spots showing the constellation shapes of Ursa Major and Minor; silver stars, each one telling a part of the Greek myth of Great Bear and Little Bear (characters: Zeus, Hera, Kallisto and Arktos)

WHAT TO DO

● This could be presented as an assembly with the whole class taking part. Allocate the roles of Zeus, Hera, Kallisto and Arktos to children who are confident in drama.

● The children mime the story of the constellation as it is read. The story is divided up and written onto silver stars - one for each star in Ursa Major and Ursa Minor.

● Read the first 'star' – the first section of the story (miming is carried out simultaneously) – and then approach the night sky (large sheet of black paper) and place the star in the appropriate position.

● As each section is read, mimed and placed in the night sky, remaining children join the stars with chalk lines to show the constellation.

THROW A STORY

THINKING SKILL: creative
SUBJECT LINK: literacy
LEARNING LINK: auditory
ORGANISATION: whole class
RESOURCES: a ball or other object that can safely be thrown around the circle; a large piece of paper and pens; collection of objects as a stimulus – optional

WHAT TO DO

● Sit the children in a circle with the paper in the centre. Create a character for a class story by drawing a cartoon person on the large piece of paper. Then write notes around the person detailing his/her name, age, where he lives, family, hobbies and so on, so that the character becomes 'real'. Now choose one child to be that character. (You could pin the drawing to them or they could hold it up.)

● The rest of the class sit spread around the room with an object to include in the story. The 'main character' begins the story; for example, *Daisy Dream-a-lot felt she needed a holiday...* The story continues by the 'main character' selecting somebody to make their contribution.

● The second person begins with the word, *Fortunately...*, adds his/her sentence(s), and then gets up to start a chain behind the main character. Another person is then chosen by the main character and his or her sentence must begin, *Unfortunately...* with a counter situation. Children can choose to include any of the available objects as they tell their part of the story.

● Alternate 'fortunately' and 'unfortunately' scenarios until the whole class has joined in the story chain.

● At the end of the session the teacher chooses the storyteller of the day based on the most imaginative scenarios, clever twists and incorporation of objects.

DRAMA STARTERS

THINKING SKILL: evaluation
SUBJECT LINK: PSHE
LEARNING LINK: auditory
ORGANISATION: small groups
RESOURCES: drama starters on strips of card as detailed below (laminate for future use)

1. *I didn't mean to break it...*
2. *Would you like a lift?*
3. *You know I've made a friend on the internet, well we've arranged to meet...*
4. *I need to borrow some money, it's very important but I can't tell you what for at the moment...*
5. *Why has Dad got to change jobs? I don't want to leave – this is my home!*
6. *The door's not locked, come on...*

WHAT TO DO

● The children create a small drama starting with the 'Drama Starter' allocated to their group.

● They decide who is involved in the scenario, what the conflict/situation is about, the points of view of each person involved and how the conflict/situation could be resolved, preferably so that everyone is happy and no one gets hurt.

● The resolution is the difficult part and will require careful consideration and discussion before the drama begins.

A MOUNTAIN TREK

THINKING SKILL: information processing
SUBJECT LINK: geography
LEARNING LINK: visual
ORGANISATION: individuals then whole class
RESOURCES: the internet, books, CD-ROMS and so on about mountains and geology; A4 fact cards (one each); scissors; glue; writing materials; chalk; world map

Fact card examples:
1. I am the Earth's inner core.
2. I am the Earth's outer core.
3. I am the mantle.
4. I am the Earth's crust.
5. I am a tectonic plate.
6. I am a volcanic mountain.
7. I am a fold mountain.
8. I am a fault block.
9. I am a dome mountain.
10. I am an erosion mountain.
11. I am a glacier.
12. I am Mount Everest, the tallest mountain in Asia.
13. I am Mount Aconcagua, the tallest mountain in South America.
14. I am Mount McKinley, the tallest mountain in North America.
15. I am Mount Kilimanjaro, the tallest mountain in Africa.
16. I am Mount Elbrus, the tallest mountain in Europe.
17. I am Mount Willhelm, the tallest mountain in Oceania.
18. I am Vinson Massif, the highest mountain in Antarctica.
19. I am a Himalayan marmot.
20. I am a snow leopard.

Extend the list as required to include mountain ranges, mining locations, famous tourist locations, and so on.

WHAT TO DO
● The children take one blank fact card each and decide what to be, individually, as homework prior to the activity.

● Draw a map of the world in chalk on the playground or hall floor. Each person stands (approximately) in the location of his/her fact card. Those representing the inside of the Earth stand in a chain on the outside. Volunteers can then take a mountain trek around the world. They choose their own route – stopping along the way to hear the fact cards being read out.

NOW TRY THIS
Present this as an assembly for the rest of the school.

WASTE ANALYSIS

THINKING SKILL: enquiry
SUBJECT LINK: geography
LEARNING LINK: visual
ORGANISATION: small groups (NOTE: as a safety precaution inform all members of school staff that the activity is taking place to ensure that any materials such as broken glass or first aid materials are disposed of separately and cannot be touched)
RESOURCES: plastic bins; protective gloves; bin bags; recording sheets; scales

WHAT TO DO
● Carry out a survey for a week of all the waste produced by the school (or by a selected section of the school such as the office, one class and the staff room!)
● Allocate different areas of responsibility to each group.
● The children collect the rubbish from the designated areas each day and wearing protective gloves sort it into paper, card, plastic, organic matter, metal and miscellaneous (for example, printer cartridges which may be a mixture or batteries) and store in plastic bins until the end of the week. Also include a litter pick to see how much rubbish is dropped around the grounds or strays into the school from the surrounding environment.
● At the end of the week, weigh the rubbish and draw conclusions about the feasibility of what could realistically be recycled and how could this be carried out.

BUTTERFLY BALL

THINKING SKILL: creative
SUBJECT LINK: science
LEARNING LINK: visual
ORGANISATION: individual
RESOURCES: terracotta pots; crocks; compost; wild flower seeds; paints; brushes

WHAT TO DO

● The children create a design for a terracotta pot that is to be planted with seeds to attract butterflies to the school grounds. First, they paint the pot.

● When dry, they can fill the bottom with crocks, then top up with compost, sprinkle wildflower seeds on the compost and then cover with a little more compost.

● Remind them to periodically water the seeds and thin out when necessary.

● Put the pots of flowers in a suitable location in the school grounds.

● Observe and record any butterflies that are attracted to the flowers. Keep a class record.

PUPPET PEOPLE

THINKING SKILL: creative
SUBJECT LINK: art
LEARNING LINK: visual, tactile
ORGANISATION: small groups of about eight children
RESOURCES: felt – different skin tone colours; sewing thread and needles; scissors; wool – hair colour shades; stick on eyes; scraps of material

WHAT TO DO

● Create a set of puppets for the class to use during PSHE and citizenship activities. The class will need to make a teacher, a group of two boys and two girls, a policeman, and parent or carer figure. Each group will be responsible for creating one of the characters.

● Use a simple glove puppet outline, such as the one illustrated below, as a pattern. The children cut out two pieces of felt, then sew

round them as shown.

● Now ask the children to then turn the puppet inside out.

● They can use wool to create hair, either embroider the facial features and stick on eyes or draw on in felt tip. They can then use scraps of material to make simple clothes.

PICTURE THE PERIOD

THINKING SKILL: reasoning
SUBJECT LINK: history
LEARNING LINK: visual, auditory
ORGANISATION: two teams
RESOURCES: a bucket for each team; photographs of everyday objects from different time periods, for example, Iron Age, Saxon, Tudor, Victorian. You may like to include pictures of beds, toys, houses, cooking implements, necklace and so on. Make a table to record which pictures you have used and the numbering on the back of the photographs. For example:

Object	Iron Age	Saxon	Tudor	Victorian
Toy	1a	2a	3a	4a
Necklace	1b	2b	3b	4b

WHAT TO DO

● Spread out all the photographs in the middle of the hall.

● Each team numbers its members.

● Call out a number and a photograph you would like. That team member runs up, locates the photograph they think is correct and runs to you.

● Check to see if they are right and the team with the correct photograph gets to put it in their bucket which is located next to you.

● Play continues until everyone has had a go or the photos are all used up. The winning team is the one with the most photographs in their bucket.

PUPPET PLAY

THINKING SKILL: reasoning
SUBJECT LINK: citizenship and PSHE
LEARNING LINK: auditory, tactile
ORGANISATION: groups of eight or nine (one puppet each and a narrator)
RESOURCES: glove puppets; scenario card – one for each group

WHAT TO DO

● The children read their scenario card and discuss as a group. They create a short play to show the rest of the class, using the puppets to put across the message on the card and develop one possible outcome. The class then discuss what they have seen and heard.

> *The group of friends has started smoking. They are stealing cigarettes from one of their parents. One member of the group doesn't want to join in but is scared of losing his/her friends. He/she also knows that smoking and stealing are wrong and wants to stop the situation before it is too late. What happens next?*

> *One of the girls in the group finds a wallet containing a large sum of money in the park. She shows her friends. They all have different ideas about what they should do. What happens next?*

> *A grumpy elderly man lives in the neighbourhood. He shouts at the children when they play in the street. Two of the children in the group decide to throw stones at his greenhouse and damage his garden. One child knows this is wrong and feel sorry for the man who is probably lonely and maybe unwell. What happens next?*

> *One of the children has seen a few older children buying alcohol from a local shop and drinking in the local park. They look as though they are having fun. One boy in the group thinks that it would be fun to try it out too. Another child knows that the shopkeeper is breaking the law by selling the alcohol to the other children and that what they are doing is dangerous. He/she scared of what will happen if he/she tells an adult. What happens next?*

NOW TRY THIS

Ask the children to write their own scenarios to address different and important issues during citizenship and PSHE education.

JUMP ROPE GAMES

THINKING SKILL: evaluation
SUBJECT LINK: PE
LEARNING LINK: auditory
ORGANISATION: groups of about six children for each rope – one on each end and four to skip
RESOURCES: long skipping ropes; jump rope rhymes such as the following:

> *Strawberry shortcake*
> *Huckleberry Finn*
> *When I call your birthday*
> *Please jump in...*
> *Jan, Feb, March, April, etc....*

> *Ice-cream cornet, flake in the top*
> *Who is your sweetheart I forgot*
> *A, B, C, D ... (continue until a mistake is made, then name someone beginning with the letter on which skipping stops)*

WHAT TO DO

● The rope is held by two children, who swing it in a loop and chant the rhymes.
● Each skipper judges at what point to 'come in' and skip, and endeavours to continue for as long as possible.
● When out they run out and join the back of the line and the next skipper takes a turn.
● The children holding the rope then swap so that everyone has a go at skipping.

NOW TRY THIS

Encourage the children to think of rhymes to help them learn or remember facts from their lessons.

CAPACITY CAPERS

THINKING SKILL: enquiry
SUBJECT LINK: mathematics
LEARNING LINK: visual, tactile
ORGANISATION: pairs
RESOURCES: a collection of ten different containers labelled 1–10 of fairly similar capacity (empty pots, bottles, cups, beakers and so on); measuring jugs; sink area; table for recording results using the following headings:

Container order (smallest capacity first)	Estimated capacity	Actual capacity	Correct order

WHAT TO DO

● Each pair puts the bottles in order according to capacity – starting with the smallest. They also guess what the capacity of each container is (provide a range of up to 2 litres).

● Once everyone has had a go at predicting the order according to capacity, pairs measure and record the actual capacity of each container and work out the correct order of size.

VENN-TASTIC!

THINKING SKILL: reasoning
SUBJECT LINK: any
LEARNING LINK: visual, auditory
ORGANISATION: whole class
RESOURCES: a large space; bright tape in two colours

WHAT TO DO

● Mark out a large Venn diagram on the floor using tape. Rather than circles, it may be easier to mark out two overlapping diamonds – one in each colour. The class spreads out around the edge of the room.

● Call out what each diamond represents – for example – red represents children who own a dog, blue represents children who own a cat. Children move to the correct area of the Venn diagram – someone who owns both will stand in the overlap, someone who owns neither will stand outside both shapes, someone who only owns a dog will stand in the red section and someone who only owns a dog will stand in the blue section.

● Carry this out for lots of factual, personal situations.

NOW TRY THIS

1. Rather than factual statements, create opinion Venn diagrams.

2. Make two statements such as, *Football should be allowed in any part of the playground* and *Chips should not be served with school dinners.*

3. If the children agree with both statements they should stand in the overlap, if they agree with neither they stand outside and so on.

4. When everyone is arranged, ask individuals for their opinions to check they are in the correct location.

DANCE DOWN THE YEARS

THINKING SKILL: creative
SUBJECT LINK: history – how has life changed in Britain since 1948?
LEARNING LINK: auditory
ORGANISATION: whole class
RESOURCES: jive music from the early 1960s such as: 'Rock around the Clock' by Bill Haley, 'Jailhouse Rock' by Elvis, 'Summertime Blues' by Eddie Cochran, 'Be-Bop a Lula' by Gene Vincent, 'Move It' by Cliff Richard; music to twist to, such as: 'The Twist' by Chubby Checker, 'Let's Twist Again' by Chubby Checker, 'Twisting The Night away' by Sam Cooke; quickstep music, such as: 'Hello Mary Lou' by Ricky Nelson, 'You're Sixteen' by Johnny Burnette

WHAT TO DO

● Invite a willing volunteer who remembers the dances of the 1950s and 1960s to come and talk about their experiences and to teach the class some dance moves!

● Alternatively, use video or Internet resources to help. One web address is www.coopjive.co.uk which provides a simple explanation of some basic jive moves.

TABLES TIPS

THINKING SKILL: information processing
SUBJECT LINK: mathematics
LEARNING LINK: visual
ORGANISATION: whole class
RESOURCES: hands

WHAT TO DO

● This activity is very useful for those who are not yet totally sure of their 9-times table. Ask the children to do the following:

> 1. Hold both hands in front of you, palms up. Starting with the thumb on the left hand, the digits are numbered 1–10.
> 2. For 1 × 9, bend down left thumb = there are no fingers to the left and nine remaining standing to the right = 9
> Put all fingers back up.
> 3. For 2 × 9, bend down the left-hand index finger (finger number two) you will see that there is now one finger standing on its left and eight ion its right = 18
> Put all fingers back up.
> 4. For 3 × 9 bend down finger number three. There are two fingers standing to the left and seven to the right = 27
>
> And so on… This works up to 10 × 9.

● Another quick check is to check that the sum of the digits in the answer add up to nine.

THE WATER CYCLE

THINKING SKILL: information processing, enquiry
SUBJECT LINK: science, ICT
LEARNING LINK: visual
ORGANISATION: groups
RESOURCES: a floor turtle; card; scissors; drawing materials

WHAT TO DO

● To consolidate learning about the water cycle, the children imagine that a floor turtle is a raindrop, create a story about the journey of the raindrop from its home in a fluffy white cloud and programme the raindrop turtle to follow this journey.
● The journey should incorporate each of the six concepts that make up the water cycle: evaporation, condensation, precipitation, surface run-off, infiltration and transpiration.
● Use materials to create the features that the raindrop encounters, such as rivers, mountains, leaves, pavements and so on. Make labels to place along the way.
● Demonstrate your raindrop journey to other groups.

NEWS AT 10

THINKING SKILL: evaluation, enquiry
SUBJECT LINK: geography
ORGANISATION: small groups
RESOURCES: video camera; clothes for dressing up (optional); one news summary slip for each group (see examples below)

> A group of travellers are removed from a local field.

> A school is selling its playing field to developers.

WHAT TO DO

● Each group is allocated a different news item on a strip of paper.
● Discuss the news item, what concerns might arise from it, who would be involved in the issue and what their different viewpoints might be.
● One person in the group will take on the role of TV reporter, and others will become characters being interviewed. Another member of the group will be the camera man/woman and there will also be a director/editor.
● Create a 'script' for an interview and record the news item. Play back to the class and invite responses.

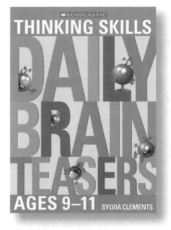